Delivering Successful Megaprojects

Key Factors and Toolkit for the Project Manager

By **Clement Kwegyir-Afful**
BSc MSc MAPM CEng FICE

DELIVERING SUCCESSFUL MEGAPROJECTS

Publisher
KAPM Services Publishing
www.kapms.co.uk

First Edition
ISBN-13: 978-1-9996664-0-8 - E-book
ISBN-13: 978-1-9996664-1-5 - Paperback
ISBN-13: 978-1-9996664-2-2 – E-book - Smashwords

Printed in the United Kingdom and the
United States of America

Publishing Consultants
Vike Springs Publishing Ltd.
www.vikesprings.com

To request Clement Kwegyir-Afful for consultation, training, speaking engagements or interviews, please send an email to:
clement.Kwegyir-Afful@kapms.co.uk

Clement's books are available at special discounts when purchased in bulk for promotions or as donations for educational, inspirational and training purposes.

Dedication

There are people who inspire you, and even in their death,
their advice keeps you going.

This book is dedicated to my Dad, Mr James Kwegyir-Afful, who
advised me to read Civil Engineering. A man who was self-taught
and rose to the pinnacle in his job. He taught me never to give up
on myself, regardless of the storms that life brings.

He died of cancer and never saw me achieve
what he believed I could be.

Rest in Peace, Dad!

Acknowledgements

A lot of gratitude goes to my lovely wife, Lawrencia, the only person who believes in and loves me more than I do myself. She pushed me to write the book.

Many thanks to my secondary school year-4 teacher, Mr Kporgbe, who kept telling me I will be a great engineer. I still draw strength from that.

Thanks to Victor Kwegyir, who gave me the tit-bits on how to start the book and keep the momentum going.

I would like to acknowledge "Vike Springs Publishing Ltd, London-UK" as the Publishing Consultants. Their patience was admirable.

I would like to thank the following people for their great comments on the manuscript: Stephen Jagger, Kevin Brown, Claire Rose, Richard Palczynski and Pratik Shah.

Thanks to my mum, Elizabeth Kwegyir-Afful, the rock of the Kwegyir-Afful family. For her, failure is never an option.

A lot of gratitude to my siblings Francis, Ernest, Andrew, Pearl and Daniella who are always there to keep my spirits up.

And, finally, the reason why I do what I do, my ultimate inspiration, my kids: Micah, Elisha, and Elise.

Thanks be to God; He makes all things possible!

Contents

Preface

Writing a book always seemed a daunting experience to me, although I really felt what I needed to communicate would help others immensely. However, something happened in my life, and I realised that, if you have something to do, then do it quickly, while you still have the opportunity.

Most people you meet these days will say they are project managers, have completed a number of courses, or have significant experience that made them 'experts'. An experienced colleague of mine defined an 'expert' as 'a spurt'. That is, a drip under pressure!

There are also several project management methods, training, and processes, so one would think that the industry has matured enough to ensure all projects are successful. However, do we even know what a successful project is? Or are large infrastructure projects just unpredictable and, therefore, success with them is rare? Or is it because we don't measure their success with the right metrics?

I have had the honour of being involved in projects worth up to £24bn and led packages worth £600m, some of which I had to guide through crisis to success. Some involved creating transition plans and changing the incumbent supplier for a new supplier. In all these large infrastructure projects, the same issues existed, and the same mindset, behaviours, and principles were required to troubleshoot them and make them successful.

This book is not meant to teach you project management principles or methods, as that is the work of the various project management institutions around the world. This book is meant to highlight some factors that will ensure your large infrastructure project is set up for success or help turn around a project in crisis. Behind each chapter of this book is a whole library of books. The intention of this book, therefore, is not to cover everything that is available or that you should know. This book gives you pointers and tools that you can apply immediately and encourages you to discover more about such tools.

In writing this book, I read several books to understand their take on the topics I cover. Although some had similar titles, I realised their content was not for the project managers delivering the day-to-day work or the package worth £1bn that forms part of the mega project. A number of these were about the set-up and procurement of major projects. Although these factors are critical, most had already been adopted by major organisations. Nevertheless, these books are all must-reads for the project leader. My intention in writing this book was to raise the critical issues that the day-to-day delivering of the project requires for it to be successful. For this reason, you may find the title of this book to be similar to others, but, I promise you, this book is significantly different.

This book, although useful for everyone in the infrastructure construction industry, is written for project managers delivering the project. It is also specifically targeted to package project managers in large infrastructure projects. These ultra-large infrastructure projects — some in excess of billions of pounds — will normally have a package as large as an entire project, with values from £200m to £1bn. These packages have their own significant challenges. The current existing literature is either too basic for the experienced project manager (PM) or too high level and intended for government officials or the CEO running the large infrastructure project. This book is meant to plug the gap for the experienced PM handling the large packages in a large infrastructure project but who is not (yet) the CEO. That project manager faces their own challenges.

From the Bible, Greek mythology, and motivational speakers, we know one thing for certain: What you expect and think will come to pass! So, for one to be successful, one needs to be very optimistic and implement great leadership on projects. Positive thinking alone may not make you an exceptional project leader; however, it will make you a better project leader than negative and pessimistic thinking will ever do.

So, be optimistic as you go through this book, for it will definitely remind you of something you already know but haven't looked at it from a different perspective or thought how critical it might be to your success.

This book starts with what success of a project really means. It reviews the current criteria for determining the success of a project and causes you to think about the actual criteria which you should be reviewing. It then focuses on the factors that improve your chances of being successful on a large infrastructure project. Leadership, leadership, leadership! True collaborative, inclusive, inspiring, motivational, and fair leadership! Although only the last chapter is titled project leadership, the tools for success discussed throughout the book require great leadership to make them happen.

The book combines critical project management techniques with insightful leadership principles that will leave you hungering for more and get you buzzing to apply them to your next project.

The book will not provide all the answers. However, it will affirm some of the skills that the reader already knows, highlight a few others, and push the reader to learn more. This is the author's goal.

The knowledge in the book cuts across industries and countries. The author believes that leadership is significantly influenced by one's cultural beliefs. However, the basic principles that affect all humans are the same. The world is becoming a global village, and no one country will have all the labour to deliver the projects in their country. The skills discussed in the book are, therefore, applicable to all cultures.

The book is also intended to provoke thinking and inspire you to go in search of knowledge to do things better next time. As Morgan Freeman said, 'I'm always trying new things and learning new things. If there isn't anything more you can learn, go off and die'.

No one knows it all. We must all, however, still pursue mastery in life and in our projects. Every day in our project's life, we should strive to do better than we did the previous day. That way, we will be successful.

Introduction

Mega infrastructure projects are vital to the future of our world and are the backbones of growing economies in developing nations. In advanced countries, maintaining the current infrastructure, and also improving it, is vital to keeping their economies from stalling.

An article in *The Guardian* said that cities are the engine of economic growth and that infrastructure development is the fuel for that engine.

The engine of growth for becoming a superpower or an established global economy is infrastructure investment. From the Egyptian pyramids to Great Britain's rail and sewer infrastructure, history has shown that to move an economy forward, a country has to invest significantly in their infrastructure. As the Middle East builds its way out of reliance on oil, it is clear that constructing critical infrastructure is the engine of growth.

China, which currently has the second-largest economy in the world, achieved that with sizeable investments in infrastructure in the last few decades.

Even as the United Kingdom implements austerity measures, critical infrastructure like HS2, HS3, Cross Rail, Cross Rail 2, Tideway, Heathrow expansion, Hinkley Point C, and Northern Hub must still go ahead if they are to remain in contention and not be surpassed by India and Africa, who are emerging global economic powers. Already, the United Kingdom has committed more than £40bn to its ageing rail infrastructure and continues to invest in each control period.

The following ten countries spent the most on infrastructure, as published on January 28, 2016, by Jasmin Cilas. These countries, as we realise, are the major economic players, likely to take over in the future if others don't keep up.

1. China — $157b
2. United States — $93.2b
3. Japan — $53.6b
4. France — $25.6b
5. Australia — $23.69b
6. Russia — $21.7b
7. Germany — $20.2b
8. United Kingdom — $16.4b
9. Canada — $15.79b
10. India — $13b

Although some of the countries are larger than others and probably have more substantial investments, that argument wouldn't hold true if you considered Japan's position on the table. It is clear that you don't become a world-class economy without properly planned and executed infrastructure. If you review the World's 25 Most Impressive Projects, you will see the number of times Chinese projects are featured in the list. No wonder they are a global economic power and are likely to overtake the USA as the number-one economy in the world.

Investing in infrastructure will not always be in large infrastructure projects. The developed world will be more interested in maintaining their existing infrastructure, whilst emerging economies will be investing in new infrastructure. However, complacency on upholding archaic infrastructures will cause developed countries to be left behind in the race for world economic dominance.

Infrastructure projects and governments will cite the creation of construction jobs as a reason why the new infrastructure is required. However, it is more than that. Top-class infrastructure impacts a country's competitiveness. It attracts business and tourism, which brings in increased tax revenue and more jobs. A survey by KPMG found that 90% of business executives said that the availability and quality of infrastructure affects where they locate their business operations. Historically, substantial infrastructure investments, such as London sewers and railway infrastructure in the United Kingdom, have been the backbone of growth in the country.

However, governments in recent times seem not to recognise the significance of extensive critical infrastructure. Infrastructure investments have become political footballs rather than what benefits the country and its future generations.

China is always my reference point, as I see it as taking over the world's economic and superpower race through infrastructure investment. It was disappointing that the Three Gorges Dam on the Yangtze River project in central China's Hubei Province displaced 1.3m people from their home and went from $8.35b to $37b. However, over the next ten years, the country plans to move 250 million people into the country's megacities. To do this, they have invested billions of dollars into infrastructure; the most iconic projects in the world are now in China. A few of their completed mega mesmerising projects are as follows (Business Insider UK):

- The Beijing Shanghai High-Speed Railway is the world's longest high-speed rail project to be constructed in a single phase ($35b)

- The Jiaozhou Bay Bridge is the world's longest cross-sea bridge, stretching nearly 26 miles ($16b)

- The Harbin-Dalian High-Speed Railway is the world's first alpine High-Speed Railway that can operate at high altitudes and low temperatures ($14b)

- The Hong Kong-Zhuhai-Macau Bridge project which connects the two vast regions was completed in November 2017 ($10.6b)

- The Su-Tong Yangtze River Bridge is the world's second-longest cable-stayed bridge, covering 3,600 feet between the cities of Nantong and Changshu ($7.89b)

- Xiluodu Dam is the fourth-tallest dam in the world ($6.76b)

These are just a few of the significant investments in China's infrastructure. Not only are they developing infrastructure that will directly benefit the economy, but the tourism into the country that the infrastructure attracts will be another source of income for the country. No one can predict the future; however, it is likely that China will be the future world leader, and they will do that through investments in infrastructure.

Saudi Arabia has a 2030 vision in which they plan to modernise and diversify the country's economy so that they are not solely dependent on crude oil. This vision is part of a decrease in reliance on fossil fuel and a turning toward a positive response to the challenge of climate change. In August 2017, prior to announcing plans for their $500bn mega city and business zone, the Gulf Kingdom launched a considerable tourism-development project to turn 50 islands and other sites on the Red Sea into luxury resorts.

These countries and many others are a shining light for the rest of the world to emulate. However, going over budget by 20% on a few of these projects is enough to cripple economies. Getting it right is, therefore, a must!

Infrastructure, when planned and executed correctly, can become a source of pride for a nation. The London Olympic Games Infrastructure, Cross Rail, and Reading Station Area Redevelopment Projects are a number of projects that the construction industry point to as successful projects.

If not executed properly, however, it can also be an embarrassment for the nation and its politicians. According to a study by Bent Flyvbjerg, an expert in project management at Oxford's business school, nine out of ten mega projects go over budget. Rail projects go over budget by an average of 44.7 percent. Also, according to a document written by McKinsey and Company, bridges and tunnels incur an average 35 percent cost overrun, and for roads, it is 20 percent.

The UK Oil & Gas Authority (OGA) document titled 'Lessons Learned from UKCS Oil and Gas Projects 2011-2016' states, 'Since 2011, fewer than 25% of oil and gas projects have been delivered on time, with projects averaging ten months' delay and coming in around 35 percent over budget.

Chapter 1

What Is a Successful Project?

Projects are generally implemented to deliver specific benefits. Therefore, a project that delivers the intended benefits is said to be successful. Some provide benefits that are different from what was initially envisaged in the Business Case, and projects that were thought to have failed, due to not delivering the intended benefits several years down the line, become huge success stories. However, benefits may not be realised for years and years, which makes it difficult to state that a project was a success. Due to this, projects can, therefore, be said to be in two phases: 1) Delivering the infrastructure to a benchmarked success criteria and 2) Implementing the completed infrastructure to reap the intended benefits.

Mostly, the client's project management team will see the project as a win if they deliver a project that meets the benchmarked success criteria. This criteria, the supposedly Golden Triangle of time, cost, and quality, has resulted in several projects being prematurely classified as failures. At times, the benchmarks were underestimated or erroneous in the first place. Note that not meeting the project management success criteria does not mean that the project is a failure, although they are mostly classified as so. One can say it reduces the likelihood of project success. Meeting the benchmarked criteria may improve the chances of success; however, it does not guarantee that the project will be a success too.

Although the client has their own definition of success, the contractor/supplier, the public, critical stakeholders, the project delivery team, and neighbours of the construction site will have their own views of whether the infrastructure project was a success.

Let's say a project is delivered on cost and schedule, but the project team completed the work while several of the team was off with stress and heart problems or the team failed to be developed during the progress of the project. Would you call this a successful project? Let's say a project completely overruns its budget; however, the final product was seen as a success by future generations. Would such a project be considered a failure?

Take the Sydney Opera House, for example. This landmark is one of the most iconic buildings in the world and a premier tourist attraction. The construction of this building started in 1959, with an estimated cost to complete of $7m and taking four years. It came in 10 years late and $93m over budget. So, was it a failure or a success?

Another example is the Channel Tunnel, a trio of 31-mile-long tunnels beneath the English Channel connecting France and England. This Channel came in at $21bn — 80% more than projected — making it one of the most expensive projects in history. At the time, it was considered a failure and, at the same time, an engineering marvel. Margaret Thatcher considered it a success, but her opponents regarded it as a failure. Time has proven it to be one of the most vital pieces of infrastructure, probably on par with the Panama Canal and the Hoover Dam. Considering the number of people using the link currently, would one regard this a failed project or has it been a success?

The Jubilee line extension started in December 1993 and then opened in 1999. The initial cost forecast was between £2bn and £2.5bn; however, the out-turn cost was £3.5bn. Although the project seems to have come in 40% over budget, it clearly had an impact. An Oxford University study in 2007 estimated that there was an increase of total property value around Southwark and Canary Wharf Stations of more than £2.1bn (above inflation), and that this could be solely attributed to the impact of the extension. The government estimated that the project cost the taxpayers some £6bn in initial costs and maintenance but has generated around £10bn of economic benefit. Was this project a failure because it did not come in at cost?

Britain is built on several infrastructures designed and constructed by Isambard Kingdom Brunel. Most of those projects came in over budget; however, can these railways, bridges, tunnels, and ships be considered failed projects if you still feel their impact a hundred years later?

Most of these projects were seen as failures, not because of the benefits realised down the line but comparisons made to a set of benchmarked success criteria, which may have been erroneous in the first place.

The fact is, advanced and successful infrastructure can cut the costs of the production of goods and their transportation substantially, resulting in several other indirect benefits to the economy. These are not typically measured accurately.

Dave Donaldson's paper "Railroads of the Raj: Estimating the Impact of Transportation Infrastructure" investigates the economic benefits from building transportation infrastructure and studying the case of railways in 19th-century India. This paper is widely viewed as an important paper in the field. To understand the economic benefits of transportation infrastructure projects, he analyses two of the most ambitious transportation projects in history. These were the building of the vast railroad system in India by the British government from 1870 to 1930 and the expansion of the railroad networks in America from 1870 to 1890. In this paper, he stated that the benefits were substantially greater than the project construction costs in both cases. He wrote; 'In the case of the US, the benefits were much larger than the hypothetical system of extended canals there — a plausible alternative use of the funds spent on the railroads. These estimated benefits focus only on the short-term movement of goods and ignore the positive outcomes on mobility of people, capital, and ideas, implying actual benefits might even be greater'. The Indian Railways, according to the World Economic Forum, is the 8th biggest employer in the world (Published by WEF June 17, 2015).

Success Criteria

Quality, time, and cost may be useful metrics for projects. However, they are not the only metrics for determining whether a project is in crisis, has failed, or was successful. I believe the impact on humans during the planning, construction, and maintenance of the infrastructure project should be one of the metrics. The new concept of the trio of quality, cost, and time triangle enveloped in the human circle should be developed. This new, fourth metric involves the effect on human factors, such as skills developed during the project, the effect on humans during the construction and planning stages, the effect on the mental health of the people building the project, etc. Who knows? Just maybe — if we focus a bit more and measure the human factor in with quality, time, and cost — we may finally be able to bring quality, time, and cost under control. It should be a 'TCQ Triangle' fitted in a circle of human factors.

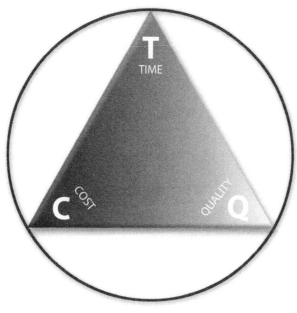

H = human relations,
mental health, development

Figure 1.1 A review of success criteria

That is to say that, T, C, and Q can move around as long as they do not affect the human factors. That is relationships among the team or parties in the contract, the development of the team, or the mental health of the team, etc.

The point is not to say that quality, time, and cost are not useful metrics or success criteria to measure against — but that they are not the only metrics that determine if a project is successful. As mentioned previously, what is considered as successful from a client's point of view may not be successful from the supplier/contractor's point of view on an infrastructure project. Different suppliers may have different opinions of what they believe make a successful project. However, each supplier will be encouraged if the project they delivered led to an enhanced image and likely repeat business if they did not suffer a loss. Therefore, to a supplier, a reasonable profit, an enhanced image, and likely repeat business can be looked at as the criteria for a successful project.

A study of four large infrastructure projects undertaken by Skanska in Sweden by Tedh Adelback and Nicolas Johansson identified the following success criteria from the contractor's perspective:

- Budget — The project finishes on or below budget

- Schedule — The project finishes on or ahead of time

- Safety — The project meets its agreed-upon lost-time accident rate

- Employees — The number of employees satisfied with the project

- Client — How satisfied the client is, which is measured by a survey

- Objectives — The objectives set by the contractor's management is achieved

- Quality — The quality is acceptable to the client

- Ethics — No ethical issues involved

- Environment — No serious environmental incidents, also set by a metric

- Media — Positive media image

Also, research on Best Practices and Lessons Learnt in Large Infrastructure Projects in Europe by the NETLIPSE project on 15 projects defined project success as: 'The satisfaction of all stakeholders'. It stated that 'perceiving project success simply as the compliance of time, finance, and quality constraints can be described as a more "narrow" view in this respect'.

Stakeholders of an infrastructure project include the project delivery team, the client, the contractor/supplier, the construction site neighbour, the users, the public, and the investors. The client's and investor's view of a successful project may be documented in the business case but not necessarily that of the other stakeholders.

Some of the criteria, depending on the project, may be more relevant to the client than others. For example, a client may deem delivering a railway or nuclear infrastructure on time as more critical than delivering on budget, due to the subsequent penalties and costs of not meeting the date. An investor's primary purpose of undertaking a project may be to break into new markets or get a foothold in another country.

The success and success criteria of a project is, therefore, not as straightforward as most people make it out to be. The project leader, from the onset, needs to agree with all stakeholders, including the supplier, what success means to them to understand what needs to be delivered. Also, they need to understand what the one critical criterion is which needs to be delivered regardless.

Note that the benefits of the project will be realised probably several years down the line; however, the project team needs a set of criteria to claim success so they can repeat it on other projects. The below are a set of criteria that the project leader can start with.

- Delivers within the budget, which includes all scope changes the client introduced with the additional budget for these

- Delivers on the agreed schedule within the agreed tolerance.

- Achieves all the critical deliverables originally set for it

- Is accepted by the client (customer and stakeholder satisfaction)

- Develops great stakeholder relationships during the project

- Ensures the team completed the work with newly developed skills which they can use in the future and are also in good mental health

- Had a successful relationship with the community which the construction of the infrastructure impacted

- A reasonable public image

The above criteria, although applicable for all infrastructure projects, will need to be refined further and tailored for every infrastructure project so it agrees with what will be used to define project success for the infrastructure delivery stage.

Success Factors

When large infrastructure projects are deemed to be unsuccessful, assessing the causes behind the perceived failure may not always be simple, but eventually, the reasons will be uncovered. Even then, the lessons learnt identification focuses too much on the lack of project management procedures and sometimes fails to identify the critical soft skills. However, determining the reasons that made a large infrastructure project a success may be more complicated. This is because the success of large infrastructure projects happens for reasons other than just complying with project management procedures, although those are important.

Success factors are things that contribute to the success of projects. There are many case studies and researches on success factors on projects in general, some specific to information technology and others case studies on infrastructure projects. I will identify five of such analyses, three of which are construction projects. One out of the three is a success factor from the contractor. Although there are overlaps, you will understand how wide-ranging they depend on the industry and whose perspective it is from. This will enable us to crystallise what I believe are the ten critical success factors that will ensure the success of very large infrastructure projects.

Pinto Slevin success factors

The following are what Slevin and Pinto identified as the 10 success factors for projects:

1. Project Mission — clearly defined goals and general directions from the outset

2. Top Management Support — Willingness of top management to provide the necessary resources during authority/power for project success

3. Project Schedule/Plan — A detailed specification of the individual action steps for project implementation

4. Client Consultation — communication, consultation, and active listening to all impacted parties

5. Personnel — Recruitment, selection, and training of the necessary personnel for the project team

6. Technical Tasks — availability of the required technology and expertise to accomplish the specific technical action steps

7. Client Acceptance — the act of selling the final project to its ultimate extended users

8. Monitoring and Feedback — timely provision of comprehensive control information at each stage in the implementation process

9. Communication — the provision of appropriate networks and necessary data to all key actors in the project implementation

10. Troubleshooting — ability to handle unexpected crisis and deviations from the plan

Jiang's 13 Success Factors for Information System Projects

James J. Jiang, Gary Klein, and Joseph Balloun wrote an article in the December 1996 *Project Management Journal* entitled 'Ranking of System Implementation Success Factors'.
This paper reports the results of a survey conducted to obtain users' and information system professionals' perceptions on the rankings of system implementation success factors. The paper lists sets of factors critical to the success of developing an information system. The 13 factors below, although written for information system projects, are also applicable to infrastructure.

1. Clearly defined goals (including the general project philosophy or general mission of the project, as well as commitment to those goals on the part of the team members).

2. Competent project manager. The importance of the initial selection of a skilled (interpersonally, technically, and administratively) project leader.

3. Top management support. Senior or divisional management support for the project that has been conveyed to all concerned parties.

4. Competent project team members. The importance of selecting and, if necessary, triaging project team members.

5. Sufficient resource allocation. These are resources in the form of money, personnel, logistics, etc.

6. Adequate communication channels. Sufficient information must be available on the project objectives, status, changes, organisational coordination, clients' needs, etc.

7. Control mechanisms (including planning, schedules, etc.). Programmes are in place to deal with initial plans and schedules.

8. Feedback capabilities. All parties concerned with the project can review project status, make suggestions, and corrections through formal feedback channels or review meetings.

9. Responsiveness to client. All potential users of the project are consulted with and kept up to date on project status. Further, clients receive assistance after the project has been successfully completed.

10. Client consultation. The project team members share input solicited from all potential clients of the project. The project team members understand the needs of those who will use the systems.

11. Technical tasks. The technology being implemented must work well. Experts, consultants, or other experienced project managers outside the project team have reviewed and critiqued the basic approach.

12. Client acceptance. Potential clients have been contacted about the usefulness of the project. Adequate advanced preparation has been done to best determine how to sell the project to the clients.

13. Troubleshooting. Project team members spend a part of each day looking for problems that have surfaced or may surface. Project team members are encouraged to take quick action on problems on their own initiative.

Chan *et al.* Success Factors

Chan *et al.* (2004), after reviewing previous work on project success in the construction sector, developed a framework on critical success factors by grouping factors affecting project success into five different categories.

Project-related factors are factors that describe the project's characteristics, such as type of project, nature of project, complexity of project, and size of project.

Project procedures consist of two attributes: procurement method and tendering method. Procurement method is described as 'the selection of the organisation for the design and construction of the project' and tendering method as 'procedures adopted for the selection of the project team and, in particular, the main contractor'.

Project management actions are actions of project management that are key to the success of the project. They include attributes such as adequate communication, control mechanisms, feedback capabilities, troubleshooting, coordination effectiveness, decision-making effectiveness, monitoring, project organisation structure, plan and schedule, related previous management experience, etc.

Human-related factors are concerned with characteristics of all key players such as project manager, designer, contractor, consultants, subcontractor, and suppliers — but, primarily the client. These factors can be grouped into two subcategories: client-related and project-team related. Team spirit is crucial to project success and underlines the importance of team building among the different participants.

External factors are the external influences affecting the project, such as economic environment, social environment, political environment, physical environment, industrial-relations environment, and level of technology.

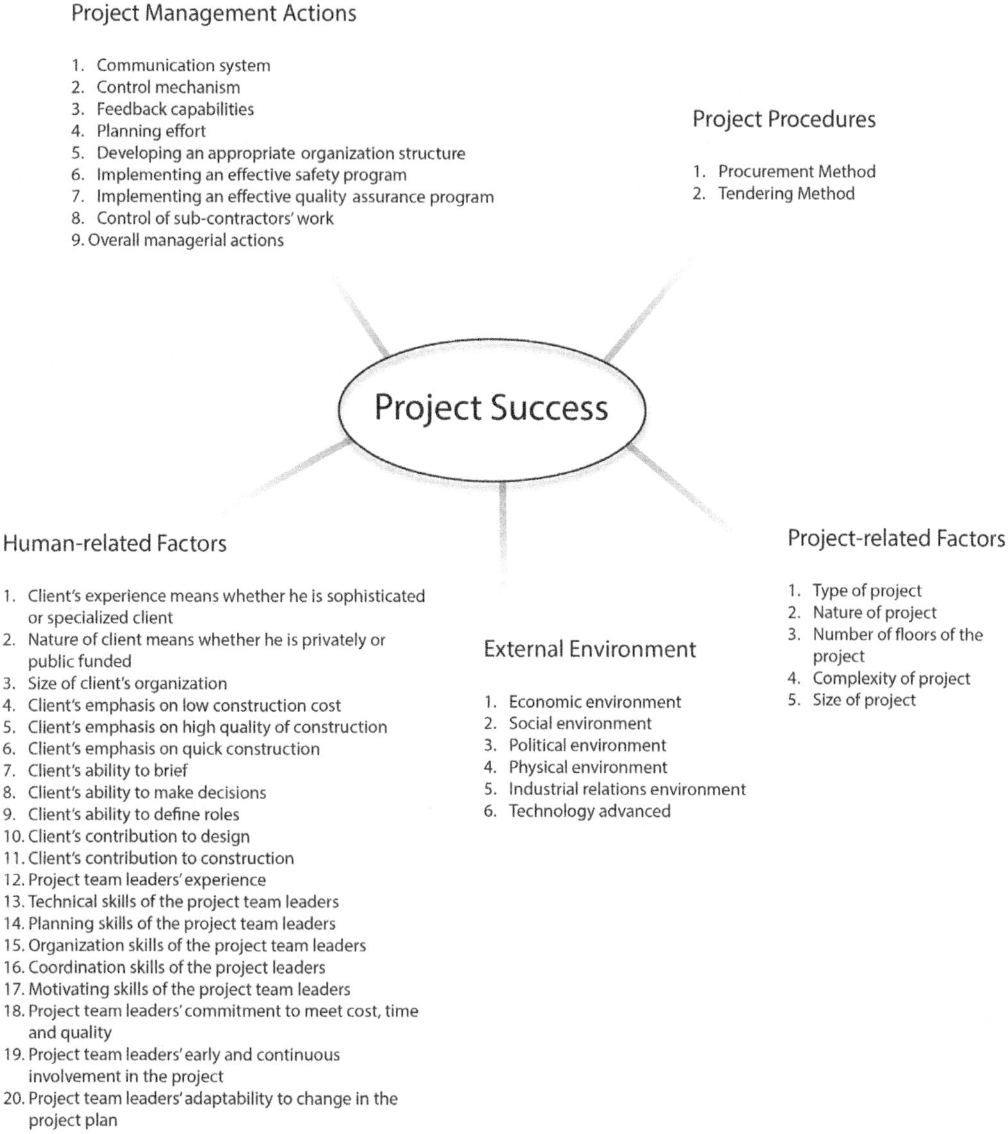

Project Management Actions

1. Communication system
2. Control mechanism
3. Feedback capabilities
4. Planning effort
5. Developing an appropriate organization structure
6. Implementing an effective safety program
7. Implementing an effective quality assurance program
8. Control of sub-contractors' work
9. Overall managerial actions

Project Procedures

1. Procurement Method
2. Tendering Method

Project Success

Human-related Factors

1. Client's experience means whether he is sophisticated or specialized client
2. Nature of client means whether he is privately or public funded
3. Size of client's organization
4. Client's emphasis on low construction cost
5. Client's emphasis on high quality of construction
6. Client's emphasis on quick construction
7. Client's ability to brief
8. Client's ability to make decisions
9. Client's ability to define roles
10. Client's contribution to design
11. Client's contribution to construction
12. Project team leaders' experience
13. Technical skills of the project team leaders
14. Planning skills of the project team leaders
15. Organization skills of the project team leaders
16. Coordination skills of the project leaders
17. Motivating skills of the project team leaders
18. Project team leaders' commitment to meet cost, time and quality
19. Project team leaders' early and continuous involvement in the project
20. Project team leaders' adaptability to change in the project plan

External Environment

1. Economic environment
2. Social environment
3. Political environment
4. Physical environment
5. Industrial relations environment
6. Technology advanced

Project-related Factors

1. Type of project
2. Nature of project
3. Number of floors of the project
4. Complexity of project
5. Size of project

Figure 1.2 Factors affecting the success of a construction project, divided into five categories (after Chan *et al.*, 2004)

Tedh Adelback & Niclas Johansson: Success factors in large infrastructure projects: The Contractor's Perspective

This case study on four infrastructure projects delivered by Skanska in Sweden, which were considered successes, identified the following as the success factors on a project:

- Establish a trust-based relationship with the client and ensure that issues are solved jointly.

- Clearly define roles within the organisation to make sure everyone understands what they are to do.

- Provide sufficient resources in the beginning of the project in order to ensure that the right decisions are made.

- Focus on technically advantageous solutions in order to build faster, safer, and with improved quality.

- Have an in-depth understanding of the tender document.

NETLIPSE Research Project Success Factors for Large Infrastructure Projects

The NETLIPSE research project, which looked at 15 case studies across Europe, identified the following common success factors among all 15 case studies, independent of the project status or national, political, legal, or cultural peculiarities:

- A clear vision and a strong political will.

- An independent and stable project delivery organisation at an early stage.

- A charismatic, highly professional project director.

- A sound financial setup from the start of the project based on a realistic Business Case.

- Adequate procedure for legal consents, with fall-back options.

- A comprehensive and systematic stakeholder management with open communication.

- A stringent change-management process.

Threats to Successful Delivery

It is crucial that in identifying what contributes to the success of large infrastructure projects, one also understand the factors that contribute to their failure. This will guarantee that the factors we do focus on ensure all large infrastructure projects can be made a success.

According to several lessons learnt from large infrastructure projects, the top-three high-level reasons that cause projects to go over budget and be delivered late are:

1. Underestimation of the project budget and unwarranted optimism about the schedule. There are three causes of underestimation of a project:

- Project leaders intentionally underestimate projects to get the project off the ground.

  There are cases in which project leaders will knowingly underestimate the project budget and schedule to gain approval for the project to go ahead. This tactic is due to some government/bank leaders still believing in

Hirschman's Principle of the Hiding Hand and Sawyer's Creative Error theories.

Hirschman (1967a: 12-13) argued that if people knew the real cost and challenges involved in delivering large projects, then they would probably never have touched it, and nothing would be built. He believed that 'the only way in which we can bring our creative sources fully into play is by misjudging the nature of the task, by presenting it to ourselves as more routine, simple, undemanding of genuine creativity than it will turn out to be'.

Sawyer (1952: 199, 203) — in a study he called 'in praise of folly', he mentioned that miscalculation of the actual project costs were crucial in getting the project launched.

Both these theories have been debunked by Kahneman and Tversky (1979a, b). They found out that optimism bias applied both to cost estimates and project benefits. Therefore, the issues do not cancel each other out but make the issue worse, resulting in massive cost and schedule overrun.

The Hirschman and Sawyer theories have destroyed careers and probably caused some wrong projects to be built. Unfortunately, some project leaders still operate in this mode and will always want to hide the actual cost of a project until it is way into construction. The solution for this requires a mind shift by project leaders to understand that some of these projects — even if their true costs are known — are highly beneficial to a country's economy, and, if they are not, then building them causes a more profitable project to be scrapped.

- Basing project estimates on outline requirements in the Business Case without accounting for adequate contingency.

At the Business Case stage, the environmental, design, and construction requirements are not fully known, and, therefore, basing estimates on these without accounting for adequate contingency will lead to the underestimation of project costs and schedule. Also, projects which involve new technology are difficult to estimate accurately and, therefore, require bigger contingency pots.

Fortunately, the UK Treasury now requires all mega government projects to take into consideration optimism bias. Other countries, like Denmark and Switzerland, have followed suit. The UK Department for Transport has a document which details specific optimism-bias percentages for different types of projects at their various stages. The optimism bias can then be replaced by an adequate risk pot after most of the project requirements are properly known.

Unfortunately, not all mega projects are government projects, and most project managers are under significant pressure to report estimates they believe are not correct, even in government projects.

- Inexperienced personnel undertaking project estimates. Some projects are specialised, an example being marine work. It is, therefore, essential to involve suppliers who have constructed similar work to help develop the estimates from the onset of the project. Spending money upfront on the right skill set will save the project a lot of grief.

The NETLIPSE research project stated that, where cost estimates are right from the beginning, financial control is normally very good. This claim was also confirmed by Sir John Armitt, who stated that the right funds being available for the Olympic Delivery Authority was one of the reasons for the success of the construction of the infrastructure required for the 2012 London Olympic games.

2. Poor execution. After coming up with unrealistic budgets and timescales, the project leaders then try to make up for this by trying to squeeze the supply chain from making any profits. The project then starts with quarrels and trying to cut corners, which affects the quality of the product being produced. Since the projects were underestimated anyway, the budget is not likely to be met, and the fighting causes the budget to be far exceeded from what the correct budget and timescales would have been. Project managers are stressed and then blamed for projects going out of control with spiralling costs.

3. Poor project leadership. This book discusses this topic in detail.

The first reason is usually beyond the project manager — especially the package project manager of a large infrastructure project. They merely become a victim in those cases.

Until such behaviour by senior policymakers and industry leaders changes, the best project managers will not save projects that were woefully underestimated and set up for failure. Underestimating the budget, which leads to squeezing margins of suppliers, results in poor execution, and poor executive leadership. This has led to the demise of large suppliers in the United Kingdom, like Carillion. More suppliers will go under if there is not a drastic change in attitude by policymakers and industry leaders.

My 10 Critical Success Factors

As can be realised from the success factors discussed, there are overlaps in them, and some also seem to be unique to the type of the projects.

Most of the success factors are standard practices on projects and are more than likely to be implemented on large infrastructure projects. There are some, however, that are critical, and if they don't receive the proper focus, the project is likely to go into crisis. What may be critical on a non-complex project may be standard practice on a large infrastructure project and not necessarily the critical factor to make it a success. For example, a robust governance may be critical on a standard project but not necessarily critical on a large infrastructure project. On the flip side, a collaborative relationship with your supplier may be critical on a large infrastructure project but not critical on a standard, straightforward project. So, the research may not always tell the whole story. Critical success factors identified in research sometimes focus more on project management procedures and less on the human aspect. The larger and more complex an infrastructure project is, the more the critical success factors lean to the human aspect, or what is referred to as 'soft skills', rather than project management procedures.

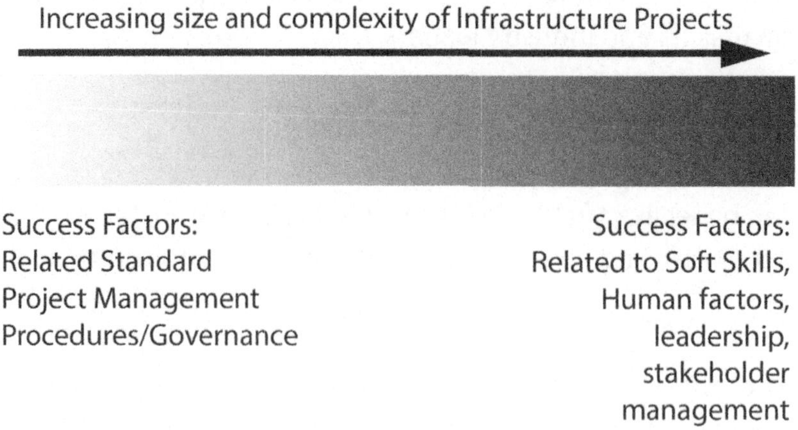

Increasing size and complexity of Infrastructure Projects

Success Factors:
Related Standard
Project Management
Procedures/Governance

Success Factors:
Related to Soft Skills,
Human factors,
leadership,
stakeholder
management

Fig 1.3 Success Factors vs Complexity of Project

As you've realised by now, one cannot list all the success factors required for every project, as most projects will be unique in one way or the other. However, one can group the various factors and consider overall success factors that will enable the achievement of other success factors. For example, if the client makes the right budget available and does not choose a supplier/contractor based on cost, then it is more likely that the contractor will provide the right resources to achieve a safely constructed product with the right quality. If the project team takes on a true spirit of collaboration, then one can expect there to be trust in the client-supplier relationship. If the contractor and supplier adopt a lean management philosophy, then it is likely that schedule and cost may also come in as planned. Lastly, to achieve all these, the client will have to demonstrate effective leadership from start to completion of the project to ensure proper communication with stakeholders and the entire project.

The 10 critical success factors identified for complex or large infrastructure projects have arrived by distilling all of the success factors from different perspectives, case studies in the industry, and my personal experience. Having been involved in some exciting and successful projects in which, nevertheless, not everything went as planned, I have been able to synthesise it all into a core focus for delivering complex or large infrastructure projects.

The following are the 10 critical success factors that I believe experienced project leaders should not lose sight of in large and complex infrastructure projects.

1. Effective top-level management support
2. Choosing the right team
3. Making the procurement process count
4. Developing a robust project schedule
5. Monitoring and control
6. Proactive risk management
7. Reactive troubleshooting
8. Supplier collaboration
9. Lean Philosophy
10. Project leadership

These ten critical success factors are the subject of this book.

Chapter 2:

Effective Top-Level Management Support

Many research and project management publications from different industries list how critical top management support positively contributes to a project's success (Besner and Hobbs, 2008; Whittaker, 1999; Lester 1998; Johnson et al., 2001 and many more). These project management studies indicate how top-level support is considered to be one of the most critical success factors in the successful delivery of projects. This support is true even more so in large infrastructure projects, which tend to be complex due to the high number of important stakeholders whose opinions carry a lot of weight for the final outcome of the project. However, the needs of complex and large infrastructure projects are significantly different from that of standard non-complex projects.

If you research what sort of support that top-level management should provide to project managers, you will come up with a long list of requirements/processes. Many of these may apply to other industries but not necessarily to infrastructure projects.

Others *will* be applicable and helpful to infrastructure projects but are in the hands of the project leader to undertake, relative to what they are responsible for and the size of the project. For example, if you are leading a £24b project, you will be accountable for ensuring that the project procedures, organisational principles, quality management, and risk-management processes, etc., are set up. If the £24b project is delivered in several packages, the package project managers, while they might remain supportive, may look to the overall project leader to implement these. A £5m project run by one project manager will adopt these processes from the parent organisation and will need top-level management support from their parent organisation. Accordingly, the top-level management support required by a package leader in a £24b project will be different from the project leader handling the £24b project — and also different from that of the £5m complex project being handled by one project manager.

Also, research shows that cultures and different countries also sometimes influence which critical processes top-level management need to focus on. The principles discussed in this chapter are, therefore, wide-ranging, allowing for applicability across the board to all the different levels, cultures, and countries. Some may not apply to a particular level of responsibility, culture, or country. Note that project management is about tailoring to fit the requirements of that project, as every project or package is unique in its own way.

In general project management procedures, there will be the sponsor or executive management who have specific roles on a project. The overall £24b project will have a sponsor who will have specific roles and so will the £500m package, which forms part of the £24b project. My reference to 'top-level management support', therefore, refers to the support channelled through this single individual assigned to the overall project or a package of the large infrastructure project.

With limited resources and less time available to top-level management in large and complex infrastructure projects, how effective this sponsor is will contribute significantly to the success of the project or package.

What Is Effective Top-Level Management Support?

There are many forms of support that senior management can give a project or many decisions that they feel they need to get involved in which, in their opinion, will be beneficial to the project. However, some of these may disrupt the project, and others may not provide adequate support to the project manager.

With all the different issues and challenges which require the attention of senior management on a project and with their limited time and resources, senior management will need to focus their time on the issues that will provide the most impact on success on the project. They shouldn't focus solely on things they are comfortable with and ignore the critical elements that project managers actually need support on to make the project a success. Focusing their energies on the right things — those that have the most impact — is what I refer to as effective top-level management support.

Not every senior manager with a vested interest in the project or package of work should get involved and potentially disrupt the flow of the project or make demands that may not be in line with what has agreed upon. The basic project management principle of having one senior manager directly responsible for the project or package of work is critical to ensure that the support is effective and not a scatter-gun approach. That senior manager, referred to as the sponsor, will ensure that information required by other top-level managers will be supplied to them in a timely manner. Note that, depending on the size of the project and who is sponsoring the project, this could be a senior manager in the organisation sponsoring the project, a government official, or a senior manager in the mega project for that particular package of work.

The project manager will be faced with many challenging situations, some of which will require a quick response to save time and money in the long run. Some of these decisions will not be popular in the beginning; however, they will prove their worth in the end. Without effective top-level management support, the project manager will lack the confidence and authority to make these difficult decisions, which could result in the project going into crisis.

Let's be frank: The project manager will not always get it right. However, they should have a leadership team that is ready to support, back, and give them the resources and support that they need.

The following are the processes or areas in which I believe top-level management involvement helps in the successful delivery of large infrastructure projects.

- Ensure the right budget is obtained for the project or package of work. As we mentioned in a previous chapter, getting the right funds for the project or package of work is critical to the success of the project. This is where the sponsor's primary focus should be. This is where their negotiation skills and leadership are required. Help set the right budget!

- Help set the right values, culture, and behaviour on the project. This is especially critical for large infrastructure projects, which tend to be convoluted.

- Develop solid relationships with critical organisations. Everyone in a mega project knows that the success of any infrastructure project is dependent on organisations such as the environmental agency, health and safety executives, county councils, the office of rail regulation, the office of nuclear regulation, and other specific organisations pertaining to that type of project. The sponsor responsible for the project or package of work should spend time developing good relationships with people in these organisations to help facilitate definitive decision-making processes or help mediate when issues come up which require quick decision-making. These relationships should continue even if the immediate requirements of consents are achieved. This was one of the significant success factors of the Reading Station Area Redevelopment Project.

- Develop solid relationships with particular stakeholders who will have significant power to influence the project. The senior manager should develop relationships — whether in the project or outside the project — with specific individuals who have the power to impact the project so they can intervene or help drive critical decisions when required. This will allow the project manager to deliver the project rather than dabble in politics, which will take their focus off the critical work.

- Help secure the right resources for the project. Some think that, once the budget is right, then the resources will be OK. However, on work packages in a mega project, human resources are sometimes part of the overall project's budget not the individual work packages. The sponsor should, therefore, help the project manager secure the resources they need to deliver the project successfully.

- Help coach and mentor the project manager if he/she can or make resources available for that.

- Help secure resources to train and develop the team in leadership and project management skills required to deliver the project.

- Help create an environment where the team are focused on continuous improvement and are allowed to challenge existing procedures.

- Help align the work package with the overall project vision or project with overall project sponsor vision.

- Help ensure that the right quality and safety are of greater importance than achieving milestones and shaving project costs.

- Help ensure that senior management in supplier organisations are aligned with the project goals set by the project manager. This should be done in discussion with the project manager to ensure the message is aligned.

- Agree on the reports required and the timing of them with the project manager.

- Defend the project team against organisational interference.

- Make timely decisions, and ensure other senior management, who need to make decisions for the project, make timely decisions.

- Agree on the project milestones and project success criteria that the project will be monitored on.

- Agree on what will cause an intervention in the project — that is, will cause senior management to get into the details of the project. This will ensure there is no unnecessary interference in the project and also that any necessary intervention is done at the right time to prevent the project from descending into crisis before senior management gets involved.

The sponsor's goal is to make the project manager successful, as the project manager's success is their success.

An example of how top-level management can help happened to John: a rising star in project management. John was a PM on critical infrastructure in the UK with high media exposure. On the project, the contractor had underbid and was trying to find ways to put claims on the table. However, because John had total understanding of the project, they could not do this. They resorted to a strategy to get management to remove him from the project. However, due to the support he enjoyed from his senior team, they backed him regardless and told the contractor that he was very capable and knew what he was doing. Those were very stressful times for John, as some seniors were nearly swayed. After a while, he was able to prove to senior management what was actually happening. The contractor accepted their fault, apologised, and removed their senior team, who were trying to deceive not only the client's senior team but theirs as well. The client's and contractor's teams came together and turned the project around. The project moved from crisis to a multiple award-winning project. This issue is not unique in the industry.

Attributes of the Senior Manager Assigned to the Project

To be able to focus on the critical things that will enable the project manager and project to be a success, the project sponsor should have particular attributes so they can effectively support the team.

Research undertaken by Jane Helm and Kaye Remington in "Effective Project Sponsorship" in the Project Management Journal is of particular relevance as it relates specifically to complex infrastructure projects. The outcomes also support attributes that I believe will enable the senior manager to effectively address the critical duties we have discussed previously. The attributes are as follows:

- Appropriate seniority and power within the organisation

- Political knowledge of the organisation and political savvy

- Ability and willingness to make connections between project and organisations

- Courage and willingness to battle with others in the organisation on behalf of the project

- Ability to motivate the team to deliver the vision and provide ad-hoc support to the project team

- Willingness to partner with the project manager and project team

- Excellent communication skills

- Personal compatibility with other key players

- Ability and willingness to provide objectivity and challenge the project manager

Situations That Indicate There is no Top-Level Management Support.

Some of the things that indicate there is no top-level management support and which should be discussed with the senior team are as follows:

1. Senior management always involved in the details and micromanaging project managers.

   This may be a result of lack of confidence in the project manager or lousy leadership from the senior team. It is essential to allow the project manager to do their job as they understand the project a lot more. Where needed, provide coaching. Too much interference will cause the project manager to lose their confidence, and they subsequently won't be able to deliver the required targets.

2. Senior management undermining the project manager by always cutting the line of hierarchy and going straight to his/her subordinates for information.

   This may seem like the senior team being approachable. The problem is, the team below will start passing information directly to the senior team and feel it is OK. The information they pass may not be a complete and accurate picture of the situation and, when acted upon, could lead the project into crisis.

3. Senior client team cutting across the project manager and communicating and dealing with the supplier's project managers directly for information.

   This is sometimes also sold as 'We are approachable and trying to help.' This undermines the authority of the project manager and affects their ability to challenge the contractor, as they will continuously be name-dropping. The senior team is likely to receive information which is not an accurate reflection of the situation and act upon it. In some cases, contractors looking after their interest may create a rift in the team to gain an advantage.

4. Project managers also cutting across their own established line of communication and not providing the senior team with the support they need.

5. Project managers not providing the right information for the specific needs of their senior team, resulting in a lack

of support due to the senior team feeling like they do not have adequate information to do their job well.

6. Senior management not willing to back resources requested by the project manager for delivering the project.

7. Senior management sending confusing signals as to whom they recognise as the leader of the project team.

Addressing Issues with Top-Level Management Support

The issues identified previously are recipes for leading the project into crisis and need to be taken seriously and addressed. The project manager should take steps to address this when he/she realises it's happening by making the senior team aware and taking steps to build confidence in the senior team. This may require the following:

1. Involving the senior team in discussions to understand their individual information requirements so the project manager can tailor reports to them. This should include the frequency and content of the reports. Note that this may be utterly different from project reporting requirements.

2. Discussing with the senior team the impact of their actions. Some may not be aware of their effects and will quickly reassess and address the issue.

3. Seeking your project mentors help to address the issue.

4. Drafting a communication plan for the project team and the senior team if one doesn't exist.

5. Drafting an escalation procedure with the supplier for the project team. This will ensure that everyone is aware of

when issues need to be raised to the senior team and the process involved in escalation.

6. Giving team members credit for their work. Neglecting this can sometimes cause team members to seek their own glory with senior management.

7. The project leader should also develop the right skills of managing upwards. They should be careful about always transmitting bad news about the supplier up the chain. This can cause senior management to feel that the project is always in crisis although it is not.

Chapter 3:

Choosing the Right Team

'Hire right, because the penalties for hiring wrong are huge.' — Ray Dalio, in his book Principles.

People build projects, not processes, and projects fail due to the wrong values, behaviours, and culture of the people in the organisation. This makes getting the right blend of people to deliver the project critically important — and even more so for large infrastructure projects, which tend to be very involved.

Large infrastructure projects require people who can make decisions quickly throughout the project. The success of the project depends on the likelihood of those decisions being right decisions overall. Therefore, the 'who' is more important than the 'what'. So, therefore, you should not be focusing on 'what should be done' but on 'who is being given the responsibility to determine what should be done'.

Some leaders recruit people just like themselves, which can sometimes lead to 'group-think'. This type of thinking ignores the various personality traits and individuals required to complement each other to create a high-performing team. Some personality traits are more suited for particular roles. An example being, a personality trait may suit an engineering role rather than a project manager role on a large infrastructure project. This is not to say that the engineer couldn't do the project manager's job. It is just that their personality traits will make them more satisfied if he/she is put into an engineering role.

However, knowing that people tend to pick people like themselves could also be used as an advantage. That is, if you were looking for a visionary person, then you will probably get a visionary person if you involved a visionary team member in the interview. Accordingly, if you are looking for certain mixed qualities, then you'll probably want to enlist interviewers who together possess those diverse qualities.

Selecting your team should, therefore, be rigid and based on the assumption that people typically don't change. Although they may be able to blend in initially, when a crisis arises, they are likely to re- vert back to who they really are. Therefore, don't design the job to fit the people. Consider the attributes and traits of the individuals and whether they fit the role. If you want a project leader who can build collaborative relationships, don't choose a project leader just because they were successful on another project. Rather consider if they have the specific traits for building collaborative relationships. Countless successful CEOs had failed when they were asked to lead organisations that required high levels of collaboration. Remember: People don't change their values much, so don't think you can train them out of it.

Your ultimate aim in selecting a team is to have a high-performance team who are competent in the specific area of the project. Below is what I believe one should consider in selecting a team:

- The individual member's passion for their subject matter area

- The emotional intelligence of the people you are employ- ing

- Their willingness to learn, regardless of their experience

- Their personality types, considering the team you are building

- The complexity of the project and what it requires

- Diversity in the team

- The feasibility of aligning the vision of the individuals you are employing to that of the project

- Consider which values, abilities, and skills you need — in that order

- Recruit for the various stages of the project

The Individual Member's Passion for Their Subject Area

'Do not hire a man who does your work for money, but him who does it for the love of it.' — Henry David Thoreau

'The only way to do great work is to love what you do.' — Steve Jobs

'Working hard for something we don't care about is called stress; working hard for something we love is called passion.' — Simon Sinek

'What's money? A man is a success if he gets up in the morning and goes to bed at night and in between does what he wants to do.' — Bob Dylan

'Choose a job you love, and you will never have to work a day in your life.' — Confucius

'We spend a third of our day at work, a third of our day with family, and a third of our day asleep. However, if we hate what we do, we will

be stressed, we will not sleep well, and our time with our family will be fraught with quarrels. Look after that third, and the rest are likely to be OK.' — discussed with a friend

These quotes sum up why passion is the key to delivering success in anything. There will be times that people are passionate about what they do but not necessarily enthused about the work you will be giving them. For such situations, you will need to ensure that you can challenge them with stretched targets to keep their passion alive. The human mind loves a challenge and is fulfilled when it solves difficult tasks.

Here are a few reasons for employing people who are passionate about what they do:

1. People who love what they do are more likely to come up with creative and innovative ideas. They are also able to look past the dull days since every project has highs and lows. Someone who is passionate about what they do will have more highs than lows. Therefore, it requires less effort to motivate the team, and you can focus your energy on other things.

2. They are more inclined to work longer hours when the project requires. All projects are filled with times when things come up, and people need to put in extra hours to complete what is required. People who are passionate about what they do are more likely to be able to do this effectively, with little complaining.

3. People who are passionate about what they do are normally able to go above and beyond what their job description requires them to do. There will be times when you will need people to undertake work that is not defined in the job description. People who are passionate

about what they do are easier to convince to go beyond the call of duty.

4. People who love what they do are more likely to find fulfilment at their workplace. This keeps them motivated and makes it easier to create a high-performance team.

5. People who are passionate about their work are more likely to push the project till they are successful. The point is they care too much to allow their passion to falter and the project to fail.

6. Passion enhances the desire to pursue mastery. Mastery, for me, should be the goal of anything you do, which means you are more likely to achieve project goals.

7. A passionate person will be an energiser in the team. They will provide energy which others will feed on; in the long run, this will make the project an exciting and enjoyable environment, helping in the creation of a high-performance team.

8. It is easier to connect the vision of the project to the vision of individuals who are passionate about what they are doing. Thus, achieving success is probable.

Of course, passion won't solve everything, and there are times when even very passionate people may feel a bit down. The project leader will need to show strong leadership to help them through that phase. Finding people who are passionate about what they do is not an easy task, as most people drift into careers they never cared about in the first place. Having team members who are passionate about what they do contributes to a successful project.

Emotional Intelligence of the Individuals You are Employing

'Emotional intelligence relates to a person's ability to perceive, control, evaluate, and express emotions'— Daniel Goleman. While those with high emotional intelligence scores may not have a great deal of technical or academic knowledge, they have been shown to perform better in the workplace than those with high Intelligence quotient scores. This is because they are more aware of themselves, better able to regulate their actions, better at owning responsibility, motivated, and have empathy for others.

Although researchers claim that an individual's success in life is determined both by their emotional intelligence and intelligence quotient, there is evidence that IQ accounts for only a minute percentage of that. The Carnegie Institute of Technology discovered that '85% of your financial success is due to your personality and ability to communicate, negotiate, and lead. Shockingly, only 15% is due to technical knowledge.'

What this statement tells us is that 85% of our success is due to our emotional intelligence. You can teach skills and grow through experience, but to change a personality type is a difficult task, especially for the short duration of a project.

For large infrastructure projects, in which different skillsets, personalities, suppliers, and stakeholders are involved, tending to make it more complex, the ability to be able to stand in someone else's shoes and understand their perspective is a recipe for success. The larger and more complex an infrastructure project is, the greater the requirement is for emotional intelligence as opposed to technical skills.

The five categories of emotional intelligence that you are looking for in team members are:

1. **Self-Awareness** — the ability to tune into your emotions and manage them will make a person more self-confident. Research shows that the more confident you are, the more likely people will trust what you say. The greater the trust on a project, the greater the likelihood of success.

2. **Self-Regulation** — You can become very combative in the workplace if you are not in control of your emotions. This will make you very resistant to change. A person in control of their emotions is more likely to take responsibility for their actions, adapt well to change, and be open to new ideas. Also, one of the success factors in individuals on large infrastructure projects is resilience in the face of change: one of the major causes of stress.

3. **Motivation** — This is your constant drive to pursue excellence, commit to the goals set, act on opportunities, and be an optimist, pursuing goals persistently despite setbacks — and there will be many on a project. Again, with the comparatively long duration of large infrastructure projects, constant change and uncertainty can demotivate people. Hiring people with built-in high levels of self-motivation makes the project leader's job easier.

4. **Empathy** — The ability to stand in someone else's shoes and understand the way they feel is a great asset. The ability to understand the feelings behind the signals someone is sending you will enable you to send the right signals back to the individual. This is critical in a large infrastructure project environment, where team members live away from home. Project requirements and family requirements can have a significant impact on their performance. Also, having someone who can see a supplier's point of view will enable him or her to be more collaborative with the supplier because the goal is to make your supplier successful, which, in turn, makes you successful.

5. **Social skills** — A solid set of interpersonal skills is key to a successful project. This will enable the individual to be a better communicator, wield more influence, be a change catalyst for the team when change is required, help build consensus, and improve collaboration with the suppliers. Also, large infrastructure projects are complex, due to the large number of stakeholders and organisations involved with the project. An individual with excellent social skills will help properly integrate everyone's needs.

It is true that personalities are difficult to change, whilst one may gain intelligence simply by using Google. Developing all of the five categories of emotional intelligence will not be achieved without some difficulty. When recruiting their team, the project manager needs to be aware of where their new team members need development and be ready to create the right structure to help in this. They also need to understand the time they have and the role the person is required for if training is necessary.

Their Willingness to Learn, Regardless of their Experience

'The illiterate of the 21st century will not be those who cannot read and write, but those who cannot learn, unlearn, and relearn.' — Alvin Toffler

Have you ever heard people say, 'I have been doing this for 25 years', and yet they are not really good at it? They have been doing the same thing for 25 years; therefore, they actually only have one year of experience. You find a 'Project Director' from a reputable contractor saying, 'This is what we do' and yet doesn't understand how to build a workable schedule or can't even control their subcontractors. Take it to the work front: You find a steel fixer not wanting to wear the required Personal Protective Equipment, and their response is, 'I have been doing this for 30 years.' Well, mate, if you have been doing it wrong for that long, then you probably don't need to be on the project.

There is always new legislation, procedures, new ways of delivering projects, new engineering methods, improved methods of working, etc. Also leadership and communication skills are vital for any project's success and critical for large infrastructure projects. You may never achieve mastery in all these things, but still, you should aspire to achieve mastery. Most professional institutions require continuous professional development, which means you continue studying, regardless of your membership grade. This is because one does not finish learning until one dies!

'The only true wisdom is in knowing you know nothing' — Socrates

In large infrastructure projects, there are constant demands to save money and cut down on schedule, which means one has to keep on learning new ways of doing things. Also, in a complex multidisciplinary project, there will be several areas of work that interfaces with yours in which you will not be an expert but will need to know enough to work with others. You may be leading the construction of all the buildings for the pipework and electrical work for a nuclear facility. You may not be an expert on the pipework but may need to know enough to understand specific interfaces to make the right decisions. You may be leading the construction of the civil infrastructure for a new railway. You may not be an expert on the rail systems but will need to know enough due to the interfaces. People who are willing to learn are normally more motivated and are more effective at their job.

Personality Types of Team Members

The Bible verse Luke 6:31 says, 'Do to others as you would have them do to you' is seen as the Golden Rule — and rightly so. However, I believe this verse is misinterpreted and misapplied. People sometimes take this literally! This philosophy could be misunderstood to mean that, if you are a self-harmer, then you should go around harming people. As in most biblical texts, context is always important. I am not a theologian or an expert in ancient writings, and neither am I an expert in the Hebrew language. However, during those days, the rule was 'an eye for an eye', which the ancient Jews were using to prevent people doing worse evil than had been done to them. The 'Do to others as you would want them do to you' was Jesus Christ's way of telling people at the time to repay evil with good. In modern times, we misinterpret this to mean, 'Treat everyone the same.' Many writers discussing personality types seem to start with the Golden Rule but then say you should not only treat people how you want to be treated, but you should treat them the way they want to be treated. Let me just say, the Golden Rule from the biblical text still stands true. The depth of that meaning is 'Treat people the right way.' Treating people the right way is 'standing in their shoes' and seeing their perspective!

There are several personality tools to determine personality types like Myers Briggs, Big Five, etc. But research shows that personality types can be grouped into four main types, and I feel that is an easy tool to use on a project. The project leader needs to understand these four main types of personalities to know what makes team members tick, how to bring the best out of them, and how to resolve any conflicts that these personality types bring. Of course, the project leader needs to understand their own personality type and their weakness. It is important to understand that no human being is solely one personality type but tends to lean towards one particular type. So, in assembling your team for the project, you need to select the right personality type for the role and also have the right personality mix for the project environment.

The personality types are:

- **Powerhouse.** This personality type is about the bottom line. They are about goals and objectives, and they thrive on challenges. They are dynamic and have an active personality. They are visionaries and make decisions quickly. These personality types are very productive and gravitate towards leadership roles.

  Their strengths are that they exude a lot of confidence and are very determined. They see the big picture and are very productive. To a Powerhouse, a bad decision is better than no decision.

  Their weaknesses are that they see the bigger picture but cannot communicate the detailed steps to get there. Their need to accomplish goals means that how people feel is secondary to achieving goals. They can be insensitive, harsh, and unsympathetic. They may rush into making a decision before thinking about the consequences.

  When dealing with conflict with a Powerhouse, it is important to be direct but also respectful.

- **Perfectionist.** The need of the Perfectionist is to be correct or right the first time. They are very good with details. These people have very high standards and are very knowledgeable.

  Their strengths are that they will research the details and are very organised. They are analytical and will research all the data to ensure they get it right the first time.

Their weaknesses are that they can be very negative and critical. Due to their need to be right all the time, they are very indecisive. A Powerhouse and a Perfectionist are, therefore, likely to have conflicts. However, a project leader with this knowledge can help them complement each other with their strengths. One can create the vision and ensure the detail is researched, and the other can make the decision.

When in conflict with a Perfectionist, be logical and diplomatic.

- **People Person.** These people are amiable, sensitive, and sympathetic people. They are also relationship focused.

  Their strengths are that they see the big picture and are calm and steady. They can see different viewpoints and align conflicting viewpoints.

  Their need to avoid conflict means that they can be seen as soft in some situations. They will sometimes sacrifice their views readily in order to avoid conflict.

  When in a conflict situation, stay low and calm.

- **Popular Expressive.** These are social animals and love to have fun. They want to be included in everything and can make the workplace a lively and fun place. They go to work for fun and love being around people.

  Their strengths are they are very ambitious and charismatic and are good at persuading others. They are energetic and creative. They are also good communicators and will lift team morale.

Their weaknesses are that they can be disorganised and easily get distracted. They can be seen as loud and talkative.

In conflict situations, focus on positive energy.

Of course, all these are generalisations, and no person is completely a particular personality type. However, people lean towards a particular personality type.

The purpose here is not to state that one personality type is better than the other. It is mainly to help you know how to deal with people who think differently from you and how to deal with conflict situations. As you will understand, a People Person will not take lightly the Powerhouse's insensitive attitude, and the Popular Expressive will take issue with the negativity of the Perfectionist.

I was once the project manager for a highly complex project with a lot of media attention with several high-profile government ministers visiting the project frequently, which meant meeting milestones was super critical. The senior project engineer for the project was very experienced; however, it seemed like he never wanted to make a decision. I virtually hated this guy's guts! I wanted a decision made today, and he wanted all the information that could be gleaned from every corner of the earth before making a decision, or so it seemed to me. Being the person that I was, this left me cursing most of the time, and I started breaking my own rules of top-level management support. I started making decisions for him. I got so frustrated I asked a coach for help. The coach took me through a model for personality traits and helped me identify that, whilst I was an extremely powerful driver at the time, my senior engineer was a perfect thinker.

Whilst my personality trait caused me to be driven towards the need to achieve goals and deliverables, meet targets, and always be optimistic to achieve targets, the perfect thinker's overriding goal is to be 'absolutely right'. So, whilst I would rush to make decisions, he needed all the information in the world before he could make a decision. Now was this wrong? Absolutely not! I needed to work on my personality to understand how to work with him. The interesting thing was that he was actually my guardian. He was there to prevent me from making rushed decisions, and I was there to make him see things in a more positive light and help him make decisions. As I became a better leader, I realised I needed all the different mixes of personality types on my team to create a high-performing team. I didn't need people just like me who, when I said, 'We will climb Mount Everest in two days,' all shouted in chorus, 'Let's go get it now!' I needed people who would make me think: Have we considered all the legislation? Have we planned enough? Have we thought about the fact that we could fail? These questions help us to prepare more efficiently and make better decisions.

The Complexity of the Project and What It Requires

What is a complex project? This is a broad topic, with people defining it in different ways. Hannah Wood and Kassim Gidado of the University of Brighton wrote a research paper titled 'Project Complexity in Construction'. This is an excellent paper to read.

The top five definition statements in the paper are as follows:

- Projects with a high interdependency between parts
- Projects with a high degree of interaction between parts
- Projects that are continuously changing and evolving
- Projects made up of many interconnecting parts
- Projects that are surrounded by an intricate environmental envelope

Most politically charged projects end up being complex. Some large infrastructure projects fail due to politics rather than poor planning. In this case, 'politics' refer to the structuring and restructuring of actual situations using other people's power or influence. The following characteristics make large infrastructure projects complex:

- Long duration from project concept to project close-out

- High public interest and media exposure

- High public scrutiny

- Complex funding arrangements

- Large number of influential stakeholders

- Immense environmental considerations

- Involvement of several government agencies

- Some of these projects introduce new technology

- Unique organisational structures, with multiple levels of authority

- Multiple parties involved in the design and construction

- Large turnover in delivery teams due to different skill sets required at different stages of the project lifecycle

- Sometimes involve the introduction of new government policies to make them possible

A complex project is, therefore, unpredictable and cannot be easily controlled with standard project management methods.

As the complexity of a project increases, you need a team that can thrive in such environments, as some people prefer order and cannot deal with change easily. This is something you need to explore whilst recruiting your team.

Diversity in the Team

Years of research by scientists, psychologists, sociologists, economists, and demographers show that socially diverse groups (that is, those with a diversity of race, ethnicity, gender, and sexual orientation) are more innovative than homogeneous groups.

The brain prioritises what seems most familiar, and what is most familiar to you is you. Anything that matches you (your experiences, preferences, values) gives you a high degree of comfort. The trouble here is that the brain creates a bias for you to favour people with similar traits to make you comfortable. When you surround yourself with people with similar backgrounds, traits, experiences, beliefs, etc., then what results is group-think. No one challenges your ideas, and so you are not likely to come up with innovative responses to challenges.

Note that diversity in project teams goes beyond the adequate representation of men, women, race, religion, and ability. These are the characteristics that you will quickly notice and which most people tend to focus on. But remember that you could be of different race and come from the same school, environments, and beliefs. Therefore, there won't be much diversity, although you may be of different races. You need to consider diversity of thinking and mixing people with great experience with those who are less experienced but who have different skill sets.

I was born and raised in Ghana till I completed my first degree and moved to the United Kingdom after a while to finish my Master's degree. I recall my background caused me to be very direct in meetings and sometimes made people uncomfortable. I remember once, whilst running a project meeting of different stakeholders, I bluntly stated how one of the stakeholders had let us down completely and that it was unacceptable. In the meeting, everyone was a bit taken aback and had worried looks. However, after the meeting, the client came to me and said, 'Well done. It had to be said, and thanks for doing that.' We never had any delays or any more issues with that stakeholder. Because the particular culture I came from was very direct, I had no qualms about doing that. Although it worked at the time, I have toned that down and have a better way of addressing this. My point here was that I brought something different to the table and did not allow group-think.

Since then, I have worked with the French, Chinese, Germans, Africans, Indians, etc. on different projects and experienced the richness they brought to the team.

Having worked in the highway industry for a while, I moved to the rail industry, who are a bit close-knit. Initially, they were not open to my ideas from the highway industry since they held the 'This is how we do things in rail' attitude. However, on my first project in rail, I was able to turn around a project in crisis using different ways of doing things from the highway industry. The same happened when I moved from rail to nuclear. So, in talking about diversity, this shouldn't be just race, culture, sexual orientation, etc. but also the diversity of thinking with people from different sectors.

Project leaders should, therefore, seek to create a project team of individuals who each bring something different to the project team. They should consider viewpoints based on personality and experience that together contribute to a deep and varied skill set to drive the project goals and form a high-performance team.

Consider How Easy it will be to Align the Vision of the Individuals You are Employing to that of the Project

Most people will have their own career and life goals or visions. These may be completely different from the project's vision. Whatever their goals or visions are, the project leader needs to find a way to tie their vision or show them how the project vision takes them towards their life/career goal or vision. When one can do this, the project leader then needs less effort to motivate the individual. Whilst putting together your team, the project leader should ask questions that will make their later work of aligning vision easier.

Consider Which Values, Abilities, and Skills You Need — in That Order

'Values', according to *The Oxford Living Dictionary, are principles or standards of behaviour, one's judgement of what is important in life.* These are deep-seated beliefs conditioned from childhood that motivate people's behaviour and which people will defend vigorously. Values, as they are deep-seated beliefs, can cause huge disagreements between people of significantly different values. One could say wars have been fought in the world due to differences in people's values.

Abilities are how people behave or think. Some people are detail oriented, whilst others think creatively or logically. Some people are very fast learners, and others can see things from the helicopter view.

Skills are learned tools that can be acquired. That is the ability to design a bridge or produce a schedule.

Whereas values and abilities are unlikely to change much, skills can be acquired. Projects that recruit based only on skills might experience relationships going sour — with your suppliers and projects descending into crisis. I have been on projects where very experienced people, who were specialists in the industry, had no interpersonal skills, causing more problems than they were worth. It is, therefore, essential to choose the right mix of qualities that will fit the role; always remain aware that skills can be acquired. Having said that, you need to determine the time you have and what needs to be done, then select the right individuals for the role.

This means that having the technical expertise is important but is, in itself, not enough to ensure you have the right person for the job. You need to think about whether the person fits the environment, shares the same values, has the right behaviour, and has the right combination of soft skills for the role. As large infrastructure projects are full of change and stress, is the person resilient under stress and uncertainty? The higher the role, the greater the importance of soft skills and ability to effectively collaborate with others.

Recruit for the Various Stages of the Project

Great people are difficult to find and recruit from their previous roles, and so you need to be sure how you intend to keep them. Due to the long duration of large infrastructure projects, turnover of great people can be high, as they go to seek other challenges to further their career. Constantly encourage them to speak up about how they feel so you can help address any issues is key to keeping them.

However, just as you need to know how to keep great people on a project due to its long duration, you also need to understand that you need the right people for the different stages of the project. A project will go through the life cycle of planning, delivering, and commissioning. All these different stages require different skill sets. A large infrastructure project's planning stage is quite different from its delivery stage, and people with a delivery mindset will normally get bored and fail at the planning stage. Skills required at the planning stage are also sometimes not suitable for the delivery stage. Although you may have a team with the right values and behaviours, you will need to transition some people out and others in at the various stages.

Selecting a team based on the topics discussed won't be easy, considering the many employment laws that exist when recruiting people. However, with careful planning and by picking a team that is ready to learn together with an effective leader, this is achievable.

Chapter 4:

Making the Procurement Process Count

There are so many procurement vehicles available today, and yet projects are still going over budget and not delivering on the milestones. There are several reasons for this; however, the purpose of this section is not to discuss procurement processes. The purpose of this section is to identify, from research and experience, some of the tools that will ensure that your procurement process contributes effectively to the success of your project.

The five main factors in ensuring that your procurement phase contributes to the success of your project are as follows:

1. Having the right budget for the project
2. Tailoring your contract model to suit the project
3. Preparing for the tender phase
4. Smart supplier selection
5. Knowing your risks and allocating them well

The Right Budget for the Project or Work Package

One of the critical success factors that Sir John Armitt cited for the success of the construction of the infrastructure for the London 2012 Olympic Games was 'Having a Sensible Budget'. He said that this allowed them to make bolder decisions. Having the right estimate for a complex infrastructure project is key to its success.

All projects will estimate the project costs before going into competitive tender. Since you will pay one way or the other for the true cost of the project, you first need to invest in preparing for the initial estimate for the project by hiring suppliers who have experience in building such projects. If the client has already informed you about their general budget parameters, it might be necessary to bring in consultants to help develop the estimates. If the client has a fixed budget, then the best thing to do is to design the project to fit the client's budget. This may require scope reduction and less 'gold-plating'. Care should be taken not to artificially reduce prices to 'make it fit'.

Bent Flyvbjerg, an expert in project management at Oxford's business school, estimated that nine out of ten projects go over budget. This, I believe, is not due solely to poor control of the project or scope creep. It may be the result of the initial estimate for the project being wrong in the first place.

The worst start a project can have is one whose costs have been completely underestimated — that is, the supplier 'lowballs' the bid to win the project. From that point forward, relationships are going to be strained. The supplier will be looking for ways to make their money back, and the client will feel lied to and have no trust in the contractor. The project is heading for crisis, and the contractor wouldn't want to take a loss. The only real option if the client wants to hit their critical milestones is either to renegotiate the price with incentive milestones or change suppliers. I have done both of these, and they are not the best way to go. I cannot stress strongly enough that you must develop a proper estimate for the project and create a procurement model that ensures that you are paying a fair price for the project. If you do not have the budget, then you must consider designing the project to fit the budget.

Tailor Your Contract Model to Suit the Project or Work Package

If you review large infrastructure projects delivered around the world, you will realise that there is no single model for contracting projects successfully. It is, therefore, unwise to transfer best practices from one project to another. There are Design, Build, Finance, Maintain and Operate (DBFMO) contracts, Alliance Form of contracts, Engineering, Procurement, and Construction contracts, Design and Build contracts, Build Only contracts, etc. Some organisations, regardless of the project or work package, will contract on a Design and Build basis so they can transfer the risk to the supplier.

The contracting model one chooses should take into consideration:

- Complexity of the project

- Scale of the project

- Sufficient capacity in the commercial banking markets for a Public-Private Partnership (PPP)

- Whether the project involves new technology

- Culture fitness in the country in which it is being implemented

- Risk appetite of the industry for the type of project

- Maturity of the client organisation

- Available resources in the industry

- Timescales available to complete the project

- Available client resources for managing the project

- Where the skill set lies — is it client or supplier?

The contracting model needs to be completely thought through at the beginning, as this is all about risk allocation and, therefore, determines the success of a project. A DBFMO contract may be suitable for one motorway toll road as a good incentivisation model but not necessarily so for another or a nuclear project involving new technology.

Likewise, a rail organisation may have more experience in delivering certain types of projects, and, therefore, a particular contract model may suit the project better than others.

Even within a large infrastructure project, individual work packages will have varying complexities and may require a different contract model than other packages. It is dangerous for senior leaders to adopt the same contracting model for all packages.

Two significant projects in the United Kingdom, both large (in excess of billions of pounds) and of varying complexities, are the Metronet contract (rail project) and the M25 Design Build Finance Operate (DBFO) which was a highway project. These two were both PPP contracts. Both contracts involved similar players and suppliers. Whilst the Metronet project or the contract model seemed to fail, the M25 DBFO may be heading towards success. The main cause for failure cited by the National Audit Office for Metronet was its poor corporate governance and leadership. The House of Commons Committee of Public Accounts Fourteenth Report of Session 2009-10 cited the root causes of the failure 'in the way devolved delivery arrangements were set up and in the Department of Transport's flawed assumptions about how they would work'.

The critical thing here is to learn from the reasons for the success or failure of similar projects or contract models and then tailor the contracting model to suit your unique project or work package, considering the complexity and the factors discussed in this section. It should never be. 'This is what we did on that other project, and so we'll do the same on this project.' Effective project management is about tailoring, and it should be applied consistently throughout a project.

Prepare for the Tender Phase

Now you have done a proper estimate and decided on a good procurement model to select a contractor, which will not be based solely on cost. What do you have to do to ensure that the procurement process adds value and helps in the overall delivery of the project?

The following are things that you need to do:

- Ensure you have a complete understanding of the project and the critical milestones.

- Ensure you understand the areas of the project that are complex to build and for which it would be wise to give the suppliers a head start.

- Develop an overall schedule, highlighting the key milestones that need to be achieved to ensure the project will be successful.

- Develop milestones for your contractor by factoring contingencies into the detailed schedule you have produced.

- Make your tender questions specific to areas that the contractor needs to focus their attention on to set them up for success.

- Get suppliers to provide method statements and construction methodology for the complex aspect of the work.

- Allow time to take suppliers through the sections of the work that you consider complex.

- Undertake site visits with contractors if applicable.

- Allow time for contractors to present their construction methodology for the critical aspect of the work to your team, and let it form part of your scoring.

- Identify opportunities to save on programmes and costs as part of the supplier submission. Allow time in the schedule for this to be presented to the project team and to form part of the scoring.

- Use the procurement process to develop a relationship with the suppliers. Use the time to set the tone of the project and the culture and values that you expect on the project. (On time, positivity, collaborative, etc.)

- Allow time to hold workshops to take the contractor through the work so they can provide a good-quality submission.

- Allow adequate time for the contractors to review the documents and provide a quality submission.

- Include collaboration workshops in the process to ensure you choose a team you can work with.

We were once told by the suppliers responding to our tender documents and process that they were the best they had seen in that particular industry. They stated the client demonstrated they understood the project in detail and made the contractor's work easier.

Supplier Selection

Several organisations have an unwritten code of selecting suppliers based on a cost-and-quality formula — 70% on cost and 30% on quality. These days, a few of the organisations may choose suppliers based on quality and technical proficiency alone; however, this is very rare. Sadly, most project managers still believe that selecting contractors based on the cheapest offer is the way to go. They fail to recognise that contractors are not charity organisations and that they will find a way to get their money back. They will underbid to win the job. Since they cannot take a loss on the project, it becomes an uphill struggle, with everyone fighting each other. Finally, you agree to pay them the extra money so that they perform — or the project fails!

It is important that the client select a supplier they can work with. Thus, it is not always about price. We all know that projects chosen on the lowest price never end well. But some clients still focus on this. The intention is not to select a clone of the client either, as that will not bring any benefit to the project. The client should select a supplier whose processes, procedure, vision, and goals complement those of the client. Selecting the supplier with the right behaviour is key to the success of the project. We know that some suppliers will talk the talk during the selection process on behaviour but, after being chosen to deliver, behaviour goes out the window. This is sometimes a result of the price being too low, and so, the price has to be set correctly.

To ensure that the supplier is not just talking the talk during the tender phase, supplier behaviour should be considered very carefully. I suggest the client does the following to ensure that correct behaviour will be demonstrated once the contract is won:

- The price shouldn't be the overriding factor. Although I am talking about behaviours, it is important to understand how money influences the behaviour of human beings. Do not be naïve to this important fact. Suppliers are huge organisations, with investors, and with only one reason for operating — and that is making a profit!

- Research and understand the culture of the suppliers. An organisation cannot change their culture over the course of just one project. What they stand for overall will dictate how they behave on that project.

- Who is the CEO and their top leaders, and what behaviours do they demonstrate in the industry? Culture and behaviours are normally dictated and driven by the leaders at the top. If these leaders are non-collaborative ones, then it is best to avoid this supplier regardless of what you think.

- What is the track record of behaviours for the leaders being offered to lead your specific project? Get references from previous clients on these people. Don't rely on references from the top leaders from the client organisation only. Get references from the project team that they worked with.

- Allow the supplier leaders to demonstrate improvement on behaviours by allowing them to give examples of some of the wrong behaviours they demonstrated on previous projects: what caused those wrong behaviours, what steps they have taken in the right direction, and what they believe they can do to remedy this. Don't compromise on this. If they are not the right people, just ask for them to be removed from the selection process if the overall supplier's ethos is promising.

- The selection process should involve workshops to enable the client to gain a deep understanding of the capabilities of the contractor's top team. This should involve real-life scenarios where the contractor's team are pushed to their limit to understand their real behaviours, values, mindset, and — most importantly — if they have a 'win-win' mentality. This will ensure that the contractor brings their 'A' team on board.

- Include the leaders with the right behaviours in the written contract. We all know that some suppliers may bring their 'A' team to win the contract and then may send you the 'C' team to run the project. However, you should also be aware that people often simply move on. So, the contract should have a mechanism for replacing leaders with the right behaviours if they decide to leave the project.

An organisation's culture is its DNA — its core identity, as stated in the Agile Practice guide. Its culture will always influence the behaviour of its people. This is why choosing a supplier with a culture you can work with is critical to the success of your project.

'Culture eats strategy for breakfast.' — Peter Drucker

Remember: Procedures and processes by themselves don't make complex projects successful, although they are critical. Behaviours, culture, collaborative and servant leadership, and the right price are key to the success of your project. These should play a critical role in the selection of your supplier.

Know Your Risks, and Allocate Them Well

Understanding the risks associated with delivering the project and allocating them to the party best suited to carry it are critical.

The contract model itself is a risk-allocation process. Selecting a Design and Build contract or a Build Only contract or some particular condition for the contract, like Lump Sum or Target Cost, all signify who the client intends to carry the risk. However, remember that the client ultimately bears the risk for the project, either through a premium charged by the supplier or through the impact on their reputation. The Metronet project is an example of a project for which the government had to finally pick up the tab.

What the client wants to avoid should be a secondary condition to who is best suited to control the risk. There are certain risks, like ground conditions, that a contractor will not pick up for a tunnelling project. So, although the contractor will be happy to take on the responsibility of controlling the risk, they will not risk taking on the impact of the risk occurring. In such cases, the client will need to find ways of incentivising the supplier to control the risk. Forcing risks on an organisation not capable of managing them will only lead to disputes, delays, and cost overruns. The client may end up paying twice — first, through the premium that the contractor will charge, and second, by picking up the tab when they realise the supplier cannot manage the risk.

The client should understand in detail all the risks (threats and opportunities) associated with the project prior to tendering the project. Make a list of these, and make a decision on which risks are best allocated to the contractor even after selecting a particular contracting model or conditions for the contract. Network Rail will typically not pass the risk of possession overruns to a contractor, as the risk premium for these will be significant. Yet Network Rail will pick up the reputational damage if the work were to overrun. Rather, they work with the suppliers closely using their Delivering Work in Possession Procedures to ensure that work is finished on time and that there are no overruns.

The overall risk registers for the project should also be included in the Invitation to Tender for the suppliers to comment and add to it. This will ensure that the suppliers have accounted for these, planned for them, and will not have excuses for them after getting into the contract.

Chapter 5:

Developing a Robust Project Schedule

Time and change are definite in life. These will happen with or without you. If you don't manage them, then they will manage you. Planning is the only thing that manages time and change. Without planning, they will ruin your project.

No one embarks on a journey without understanding the route they will use to get to their destination. However, at times on a project, an accepted schedule may not exist. Some conditions of contract, like the NEC, naturally lend themselves to a programme being in place. However, these programmes are sometimes put together without any proper challenge from the project team.

If you needed to be at a place on time, you will give yourself the best possible chance for arriving there by checking alternative routes to identify the best possible route, allow for traffic, accidents, etc. You will check your engine oil, check your tire pressure, water, etc., to ensure that you eliminate — or, at least, minimise — factors which could prevent you from being at the place on time. Of course, this depends on the level of importance you place on the appointment. The same reasoning applies to developing a robust programme for your work. The programme is the route map to your destination;

how much effort you put into it will determine whether you reach your destination on time successfully or not.

'If you fail to plan, you are planning to fail.' — *Benjamin Franklin*

In developing a robust programme, you will need to go through the same process as you would in developing your route when you are travelling to a destination!

To develop a robust programme, you need to do the following:

1. Understand the scope of your project completely, and break it down into manageable deliverables.
2. Design a work breakdown structure early and stick to it.
3. Understand the areas of your scope that are complex.
4. Read up on lessons learnt from similar projects.
5. Develop written mitigation plans.

Understand the Scope of Your Project Completely, and Break it Down into Manageable Deliverables

To be able to develop a robust schedule, the project manager needs to understand the entire scope of the work they are required to deliver. This may seem obvious, but often, project managers are not clear on what they need to deliver. Of course, your scope is required to be in the project manager's brief and also the project management plan that you will develop. However, you will need to ensure that your understanding of the scope is the same as that of the sponsor and other stakeholders.

One of the classic reasons for project failures is differing interpretations of the scope by the sponsors and project manager.

The project manager will need to have a workshop with the sponsor and other stakeholders to review their scope and deliverables (tangible and intangible). They will need to identify the objective of the project first, as this will focus attention on what is really needed as opposed to being 'nice to have'. Working back from the objectives, the required deliverables will then be agreed upon. The Kano model for product development can be used to achieve this.

The PM will then put together a team with experience in the type of project to be delivered. In a workshop, they can further break down the required deliverables into sections that the project can be planned on. The team will also need to think about other deliverables that will enable the final outputs to be delivered. For example, to build a bridge, one will require a site survey, design, geotechnical investigations, etc. All these will need to be identified before a plan to deliver these can be developed.

Design a Work Breakdown Structure Early and Stick to it

This will ensure that pioneering and building in change is much easier if everyone calls 'Foundation – A' the same name throughout the various phases of the project.

Understand the Areas of Your Scope That Are Complex

This understanding is essential. To develop a robust schedule, you need to understand the complex build areas so you can use a wider experience pool to review those aspects of the work.

During the construction of the civil work which formed part of the Reading Station Area Redevelopment Project, two key areas that were complex were the Reading West Curve Bridge Replacement and the Reading West Curve Box, which formed part of the 2km Elevated Railway.

The Reading West Curve Bridge Replacement involved the replacement of an existing brick arch bridge with a concrete portal bridge in a 101-hr possession. This included removing the tracks and reinstalling them in time for freight trains to use after the 101-hr possession. As you can understand we had Geotechnical Investigation Report, but one can't predict exactly what the brick arch was founded on, and so, we were not 100 percent sure if our design foundation would be perfect. Due to the criticality and importance of this scope of work, the planning involved all the subcontractors in workshops running through the plan and tweaking it several times. It required us installing trial piles close to the bridge to give us an indication of drive rates. We had spares of everything. We had to review and tweak the design to account for any unforeseen circumstances for the foundation design. We had site layouts that ensured that the demolishing work would be flawless. We had engineers on standby, ready to recalculate foundation parameters if the conditions were different. This actually happened, and the brilliant engineer was able to solve and recheck his parameters with the exact conditions onsite. Of course, this project was successful and went on to win several awards. However, it was successful only because we understood that it was complex and because we applied the right focus and energy.

Reading West Curve Box involved beams being installed over railway lines and walls between two live tracks, with some of them 2 metres away. There was not much land to place equipment to undertake the extensive piling work. Some of the work involved very short railway possessions, and others had to be done with trains running. This meant the planning of this work had to start in detail several years before we even got suppliers on board. The complexity, therefore, influenced the choice of design. The procurement process involved specific questions on construction methodology and several presentations to the suppliers so they understood the complexity of that section of the work. The presentations included several site visits as well so they could appreciate site environment. Also, the team was able to highlight specific constraints of the site.

The complexity of the work meant that the programme development for this aspect of the work involved designers, temporary work designers, railway possession teams (so we could understand what was and wasn't accepted on the railway considering safety), specialist lifting subcontractors, specialist falsework providers, specialist reinforced concrete subcontractors, the tier 1 contractor, and client team. A robust programme was able to be built with the advice from all these teams. The overall project was completed on schedule and was a great success.

Read Up on Lessons Learnt from Similar Projects

Lessons Learnt is a backbone of project management; however, no one wants to learn lessons. Most people want to come up with novel ideas. I am all good with doing things differently, and I actually push for that. However, any unique ideas should be built on other people's successes and failures.

In developing a robust schedule, one needs to seek out similar projects to understand how they were planned and how long it actually took to complete the work. If that is different from your timescale, then you need to understand why yours is different and what caused the longer or shorter duration. You need to understand what went wrong or well on such projects and what mitigation measures they had or didn't have in place.

If you can, speak to the people who worked on a similar project. Invite them to workshops, if possible, so that they can advise you on your programme. I once had a teammate who was assigned to a project similar to one I had managed previously. It was a complicated project, and instead of my colleague seeking direct knowledge from me, he went online to watch videos of the project. In delivering a project, ego shouldn't have a place. Your focus should be delivering the project successfully, and you should seek lessons from anyone who can help make the project a success.

Develop Written Mitigation Plans

After developing a first-draft schedule, I propose you hold several 'deep dives' to review the programme with people with specialised experience in that particular area of work. You need people involved in the project as well as those who are not. You need people who have no expertise in the area of your project as well. This ensures that the project programme is challenged from different perspectives, which will disrupt group-think and secure diversity of opinion.

Some issues that may be thrown up during the deep dive which you can resolve by either increasing resources, effort, and duration or by changing how the operation or the activity will be undertaken. During the deep dive, you need to identify all the critical issues that, if they go wrong, will make it difficult to bring the programme back on track. You will need to brainstorm with a smaller team to produce mitigation measures for these issues. These mitigation measures or plans should be documented and the resources required to implement the mitigation measures planned for.

Chapter 6:

Monitoring and Control

'No battle plan survives contact with the enemy.' — *German military strategist Helmuth von Moltke*

I know that it might appear strange that I take a chapter to discuss the importance of developing a robust plan, and then, right in the next chapter, I seem to imply that relying on the plan may lead your project to fail. Planning ensures that you have a roadmap and allows you to deal with surprises better. It also ensures that you have a path that you can measure your progress against, enabling you to bring the progress closer to the original plan.

With large infrastructure projects, change and uncertainty are rampant, and the issues that can cause your plan to derail are many. When your plan meets the real world, the real-world environment forces your plan to conform to it.

In the example project I discussed previously, which involved replacing an existing bridge within a 101-hr possession, we had planned this project to 'perfection', or so we thought. The day before the work started, there was a very heavy downpour, which affected steel strengthening plates we had placed on the road for the self-propelled modular transports. Also, the ground condition that was anticipated by the geotechnical investigation was not what was encountered. So, two days into the 4-day rail possession work, we were already behind schedule by 17 hours. When our weather-related troubles seemed to be over and we were finally laying the track, some equipment broke down. Although the supplier didn't think we needed a spare of the equipment, we had obtained one from another supplier on the project and had it as a backup. All these issues came up. However, because we had a robust plan with written mitigation measures, we were able to recover and still finished on time!

So, because your plan is likely to cave in to fit the real world, monitoring your plan is key so you can control the situations that arise. You should not develop a robust plan, stick it in the drawer, and do something else. Some suppliers develop a plan and then state that the plan was only for the client's convenience and that now they are building to something else. Fortunately, conditions of the contract like the NEC ECC requires the plan to reflect how the work will be constructed.

Also, on a project, the work activities of the plan itself may be affected, or interfaces may cause the plan to deviate. Therefore, you must monitor both the plan itself and the interfaces to ensure you react to these appropriately.

The project leader needs to have detailed knowledge of the project status to understand the major risks and identify when the project is going into crisis and requires critical decisions to put it back on track. To do this, the project leader needs to have exceptional metrics that can inform their decision-making.

The Plan

The level to which you monitor a plan and the tools you use are dependent on how critical meeting the completion date is and what the overall duration of the project is. For example, you wouldn't monitor a bridgework in a 90-hr rail possession the same as you would a 1-yr viaduct package or a 4-year project.

Your plan for monitoring a 90-hr rail possession project may be every 15 mins, checking progress on the quantities installed against what was planned. This also depends on how complex your project is. Although, the widespread perception is that engineering work is frequently overrun in the rail industry, causing delays to trains. Compared to the thousands of engineering work that is undertaken over the course of a year, there are actually few engineering projects that are overrun. Network Rail has very robust processes for delivering work in blockades; if you follow them stringently and add the advice in this book, you are likely to be successful.

Before you can monitor a plan, you need to set up a baseline using the various project management advice on setting up a plan, together with the advice on setting up a robust plan in the previous chapter. Your monitoring and control are then undertaken against the baseline plan you have in place.

There are several ways of monitoring a plan which you can study in APM Knowledge, especially 'Planning, Scheduling, Monitoring, and Control: The Practical Project Management of Time, Cost, and Risk'.

A few of the methods for monitoring and control of projects from the above document are listed below:

- Drop-line method

- Activity-weeks method

- Milestone monitoring

- Line of balance

- Resource monitoring

- Quantity tracking

- Network analysis and measurement of float usage

- Earned Value Analysis

All these methods have their strengths and weaknesses. However, the ones I find most useful in monitoring large infrastructure and complex projects are:

- Milestone monitoring

- Quantity tracking

- Network analysis and measurement of float usage

- Earned Value Analysis

I recommend the use of all four methods on all large infrastructure or complex projects. This is because the strengths of one will work to decrease the weaknesses of another.

Milestone Monitoring

The way to make milestone monitoring work is by doing the following:

- Create milestones that reflect the natural construction nature of the project. For example, if it is a bridge construction project, then you will have site clearance, foundation work, piers, deck, waterproofing, etc.

- Identify the activities that are critical for handover. You won't be choosing completion of security fence if that is not essential for the project handover. That is, the milestones need to reflect the definition of 'completion' agreed upon by the client and contractor.

- Ensure the duration between each milestone is reflective of your level of control. Depending on the package leaders you have on the project, you will monitor at a certain level — one that feeds into your milestone. Also, you need to consider how much work is accomplished in a month: Do you need a milestone every month or one every week? These are dependent on the duration, type of project, and how critical some activities are to the project.

- Choose milestones that reflect both start and completion of activities. To ensure the critical activities that drive the programme don't slip too much before you produce corrective measures, it is best to use both their start and completion dates as milestones. For example, the start and completion of piers pile cap on the critical path will be milestones. This way, if something is delaying the launch, it can be addressed.

- Ensure the milestones are adequately defined and that the person who is delivering them understands them in the same way as the one who created them. Completion of milestones always needs defining so that there are no ambiguities when they are achieved.

- Ensure milestones cover the whole scope of work. Covering the entire scope of work is tricky. However, you can place your milestones in such a way that the achievement of specific activities naturally ensures that the full scope is being delivered.

Quantity Tracking

Most construction projects involve quantities that can be easily tracked, like piles, volume of earth moved, volume of concrete poured, number of pile caps completed, etc.

This method of tracking works best if the estimate of the quantities is as close to reality as you can get. This gives you a scale of what is achievable and enables you to plan mitigation measures. For example, if you are managing a project that requires pouring substantial volumes of concrete, you may create a concrete skyline to track the concrete you are pouring on a weekly basis. Let's say your plan is to pour 500 cubic metres the current week and 200 cubic metres the following week; however, you achieve only 250 cubic metres the first week. This count implies that to achieve the programme, you need to pour 450 cubic metres the following week. This method begins to give you the scale of the endeavour, and you start asking questions such as: If you haven't achieved a particular volume before in a week for a couple of months, what are the chances that you can ever reach this or the ever-increasing backlog of piling volume? You then start identifying the causes of the problem and what can be done to attain these volumes. First, if you are using a concrete supplier and you don't have your own batching plant, can the supplier meet the demands, considering their other commitments? Are the bottlenecks due to the steel fixers or carpenters? You then need to troubleshoot to identify the main cause of not hitting the goals and what can be done. It can also be that the previous plan may have been over-optimistic.

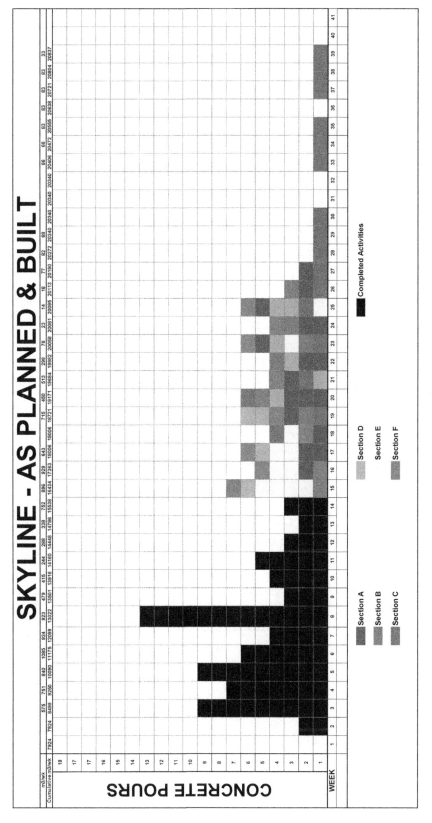

Figure 6.1 – Sample Concrete Skyline

Network Analysis and Measurement of Float Usage

A project manager should always understand and know what the critical path of their project is. You should always understand how much float you have on your key milestones and what activities drive this.

As a project manager, you need to be monitoring your float constantly. You need to continually be requesting a network analysis to understand what activities have become critical so you can control these or look for mitigation measures. Monitoring only the critical activities can cause you to lose sight of the subcritical activities. Therefore, you need to ask for all subcritical activities, understand how these can also become critical, and monitor them as well.

Earned Value Analysis

Every large infrastructure project should use Earned Value Analysis. APMs Earned Value Handbook (APM 2013) gives a detailed exploration of Earned Value Management (EVM).

The PMBok 6th Edition defines EVM as 'a methodology that combines scope, schedule, and resource measurements to assess project performance and progress'.

Earned Value Management is resource intensive and requires a lot of time upfront to set up a robust baseline. There should also be a robust and effective change-control system to protect the baseline. However, once it is set up, it provides an early-warning system, allowing corrective action to be carried out to prevent a project from going into crisis.

EVM can help you with questions like:

- Are we ahead of or behind schedule?

- When is the forecast completion date?

- What is the likely out-turn cost of the project?

- How efficiently are we using our resources?

- What is the forecast cost for completion?

When EVM indicates that the project is underperforming, you can then use it to:

- Spot where the problems are occurring

- Know what effort or cost is required to bring it back on track

- Determine whether the problems are critical or not

The purpose of EVM is to provide you with data so that the project leader can make educated decisions. Some projects focus on generating data and forget that the purpose of data is for you to use it to make decisions to prevent the project from going into crisis. But do not take the data as gospel; delve into it to understand the reasons.

For example, we had a scheduled performance index (SPI) that was way below 1, which meant we were not going to deliver on time. After delving into the detail, we realised that the completion of safety fencing had been weighted similarly to that of placing bridge beams on another package. On this project, completing the boundary safety fence was not critical, as it did not determine whether trains could use the bridge or not.

Using EVM with the NEC Engineering Construction Contract (NEC ECC) can be said to be challenging. The main difficulty being the contractor will not accept being asked to produce earned value metrics based on the first accepted programme when changes (Compensation Events) have been instigated by the employer. So, although using the first accepted programme as a baseline for EVM purposes may be great for the client, the resulting Cost Performance Index and SPI may wrongly indicate that the contractor is underperforming. Using the latest accepted programme could also lead to complications as the EVM data may have to be re-baselined whenever a new programme is issued and accepted. A solution that will be acceptable to both parties is using the accepted programme which resulted due to a compensation event to re-baseline the EVM data. A rigorous governance concerning changes to baseline via change control will enable EVM to be used alongside the NEC Engineering and Construction Contract. The important thing is to understand the purpose of EVM as a tool that helps with decision making. There are lessons that can be learnt from the 2012 London Games construction project. This successful project used EVM alongside NEC ECC. The project stated that EVM was pivotal in the successful programme controls used for the project.

Earned Schedule (ES), which is an extension of the practice of EVM, is gaining popularity. Some projects now prefer to use ES to focus just on the schedule rather than final budget estimation. The EVM schedule variance measures (earned value - planned value) are replaced with ES and actual time (AT). This means if ES-AT is greater than zero, then the project is considered to be ahead of schedule. The SPI is calculated as ES/AT. The ES theory, similar to the EVM theory, also provides formulae for estimating the project completion date by using earned schedule, actual time, and the estimated schedule.

Whereas EVM tracks schedule variances in units of currency, earned schedule tracks this in units of time, making it more understandable. Also, using EVM, a project is said to be on time if the schedule variance is 0 and the SPI is 1. This gives the impression that a project has performed well — even if it was woefully late on completion, as the SPI at completion will be 1 and the schedule variance will be 0. This anomaly is corrected by using earned schedule. Earned Schedule may, therefore, be a better theory to use for large infrastructure projects.

Interfaces

Most large infrastructure projects are made complex due to the several interfaces involved. These interfaces may be external or internal to the project. 'Internal' refers to projects which comprise several work packages, which are significant in themselves. An example is the Hinkley Point C Project, where work packages that make up the project could be worth a billion pounds and managed by a project manager. The same can be said of projects like High Speed 2 (HS2), Crossrail, etc.

'External' refers to work with external organisations. The HS2 project has several interfaces with the existing United Kingdom rail operator.

These interfaces, whether internal or external, need to be identified, tracked, and effectively managed.

A Responsibility Accountability Matrix, developed from a detailed work breakdown structure and organisational breakdown structure, will identify who is responsible for what and the interfaces between two work packages when considering internal project interfaces.

Milestone Definition Sheets are a good way of clearly defining what the deliverables are and the dates when these are required. It is also essential at this point to highlight to all parties the financial and schedule impact of these if not delivered on the said dates. This is critically important on large infrastructure projects, where your colleagues managing other packages may be your customers and critical stakeholders. Milestone Definition Sheets should contain the following information:

1. Description of milestone
2. Ownership
3. Responsible work-package leader or project manager
4. Delivery dates
5. Deliverables
6. Impact if not achieved — schedule, cost, etc.

External interfaces can be clearly identified by agreeing with stakeholders on the project scope. It is important to document what the project's deliverables are at the interfaces and the dates those deliverables will be expected.

Not all interfaces will be activities related. Some interfaces are formed from actions, documents, etc. that bring together parties of the project. This type of interface can be managed by setting up an Interface Matrix (IM). The IM is a listing of the actions, documents, or anything else which requires either approval by or communication with the various internal and external stakeholders of the project.

Chapter 7:

Proactive Risk Management

'Intellectuals solve problems; geniuses prevent them.' — *Albert Einstein*

The main purpose of risk management is to increase the likelihood of completing the project safely within the timescales, budget, and cost. As projects are, in effect, bringing about change, risks are, therefore, inherent in them. The more complex a project is, the greater the risks associated with delivering them safely within the timescales, budget, and cost.

Some people think risk management is a waste of time and have written articles about this. However, these articles do not seem to define or understand what a 'risk' is and what the risk-management process is. I am sure these people do not get up one day and decide to go off on a family holiday with kids without planning. Once you plan that event, you are basically undertaking risk management.

David Hilton, 'The Risk Doctor', has written a great article on 'The 10 Myths of Risk'. Number 2 is on risk management, and the myth is 'Most risks are outside our control, and we shouldn't waste time trying to address them in advance. Instead, we should rely on firefighting, dealing with issues as they arise. The good project manager is a hero or heroine who can handle any crisis as and when it happens — Myth!' He goes on to state, 'In reality, risk management provides a forward-looking radar we can use to scan the uncertain future to reveal things that could affect us, giving us sufficient time to prepare in advance. We can develop contingency plans even for so-called uncontrollable risks and be ready to deal with likely threats or significant opportunities.'

The purpose of risk management is to ensure that risks are proactively identified, assessed, controlled, or managed so that the project has a greater likelihood of achieving its objectives within the stakeholders' agreed-upon limits.

Risk management is, therefore, planning for success. If your risk register has the right risks and plans on them, you tend to review them on a frequent basis to understand how you are doing on your plans. It forms part of your monitoring and control of the project, and decision-making is then based on them.

The International Journal of Project and Business Risk Management, Volume 1, 1997, identifies several benefits of risk management, some of which are listed below:

- Enables better informed and more credible plans, schedules, and budgets

- Increased chance of project success

- Leads to the use of the most suitable type of contract

- Allows a more meaningful assessment and justification of contingencies

- Discourages acceptance of financially unsound projects

- Generates metrics for use on future projects

- Enables an objective comparison of alternatives

- Identifies and allocates responsibility to the best risk owner

- Improves corporate experience and general communication

- Leads to a common understanding and improved team spirit

- Focuses project-management attention on the real and most important issues

Complex infrastructure projects have several interfaces, several stakeholders with large teams, either suppliers or clients, joining and leaving the project continuously. They are prone to several changes during their lifecycles and, therefore, are very risky ventures. For these projects to be successful, the risk management on the project must be effective. To enable risk management on such projects to be effective, one will need to consider the following:

1. Treat risk management as a lifecycle process
2. Create a useful risk register
3. Don't forget opportunities
4. Understand the different types of risk registers on a project
5. Make risk management the basis of your decision-making process

Treat Risk Management as a Lifecycle Process

One of the main reasons that complex infrastructure projects go over budget and are late is the wrong approach to risk management. Risk management determines everything from initiation stage to operational stage. At the initiation stage, the sponsor client will need to understand their appetite for risk in order to understand how the project will be approached. During the planning stage, one will need to understand the risks involved in the project, which means a detailed risk identification, enabling a robust budget to be developed for the project. To understand the procurement model and risk allocation, again, one will need to understand the risks that one is facing on a particular project. During delivery of the project, you will need to continue with your risk identification and implementation of your control measures to ensure that the project is a success.

The risk-management process should, therefore, follow the lifecycle of the project. This means that, regardless of the project, a risk register ideally should be developed from the initiation stage of the project. This register, preferably a database, should be developed and continually updated throughout the lifecycle of the project. However, it is rare to join a project at the delivery stage, pick up a risk register that was developed at the planning stage, and discern the reasons for certain decisions. Ideally, the risks of the project should be driving the decisions on the project.

Typically, the risks that appear in any given phase were likely created in the previous phase. Once you decide the procurement model and conditions of the contract to use, the risks that need to be controlled in the delivery stage are set. If it is a Build Only contract, the design you complete and tender for construction will determine many of the delivery risks that you will face. Once you get into delivery, most of the work you undertake on threats are control. The first step in your risk process stage is 'Avoid' for threats and 'Exploit' for opportunities. For your project to be successful, 70% of the risk-management work must be undertaken at the initiation and planning stages. This is where you make the critical decisions of determining your budget, choosing your contract model, the conditions of the contract you want to use, the project structure, etc. Risk management should be at the centre of project selection, planning, designing, procurement, and implementation.

Risk management should be everyone's business, including all stakeholders. At each stage of the project, the project team should be considering the following:

1. What risks does the project face currently?

2. What are the potential costs of the risks?

3. What decisions that affect the risk profile need to be made?

4. Who needs to be involved in any decisions that will affect the risk profile?

5. What are the likely consequences of decisions made now on later phases?

6. What high-level risks should be allocated to the various stages?

7. Who is best placed to control each risk?

8. What sort of mindset and behaviours are best to make the risk management effective?

9. Is the current risk process on the project adequate in managing the risk, or does it need to be strengthened or changed?

10. Are our risks driving our decision-making, or are our decisions creating more risks?

The APM body of knowledge considers a typical project lifecycle to be Concept, Definition, Development, and Handover/Closure. Other publications will consider these as Initiation, Planning, Execution, and Closure. Although these seem to be similar, what some publications mean by 'planning' is not the same as the APM's definition. Other publications then insert another phase, 'procurement'. However, procurement is part of the development stage. Therefore, the activities you decide to undertake in each stage also affect your risk profile.

Depending on how a project is delivered, the different stages of the lifecycle sometimes overlap. The project may be part of a larger programme, the lifecycle finishes at Handover, and the programme deals with the benefit-realisation stage. Also, a project lifecycle may mean different things to different people. For a contractor or supplier, the project lifecycle may just be the delivery stage or may include some benefit realisation if it is a DBFO.

Using the *APM Knowledge* project lifecycle, we can explore some of the risk decisions that need to be considered at each stage.

Concept Stage

At the concept stage, where you consider the viability of the project and whether you should invest in the definition stage, you will need to consider the overall risks that this project is likely to introduce. At this stage, you should consider the following before deciding to proceed to the next stage:

- What are all the potential sources of risk that the project faces?

- What can external participants to the project do to help with information and solutions to the likely risks?

- What political, environmental, and financial risks are you are likely to face?

- Who are the best stakeholders to be made accountable for those risks?

- What risks will be introduced if we commit to the next stage?

- How is this project going to be financed, and what risks will that introduce?

A risk register, even if it is a high-level one, should be developed with a view toward driving the decisions in that stage.

Definition Stage

At this stage, where the preferred solution is identified and ways of achieving it are refined, the following should be considered:

- How are you going to develop an integrated approach and an organisational structure that ensures sound decision-making and the free flow of information among all stakeholders (external and internal) throughout the project lifecycle?

- What will suppliers be asked to design and build?

- What risk governance are we going to implement?

- What is the risk culture we want on the project?

- What are the selection criteria for suppliers?

- What conditions of contract do we intend to use on the project?

- How do we intend to manage suppliers to deliver the project?

- Are we going to split the project into a number of packages, and, if so, what criteria are we going to use to split the packages?

The decisions made here will introduce some risks into the project. Each decision made needs to consider the risks it is introducing and properly documented. The risk register from the concept stage should be expanded here. The value of the risks should be determined and included in the project budget.

It is important at this stage to have a central risk-management team who are separate from the future delivery team. This will ensure that risks are looked at collectively and objectively, without delivery-team project managers influencing them. This team will also ensure that all risks from the various stages of the project are captured and reviewed at each stage.

Development Stage

This is the stage in which the project-management plan that is developed in the definition stage is put into action. This stage is often broken down into two main stages. The first stage can be referred to as the procurement phase and the second as the construction/ delivery phase.

Procurement Phase

At this point of the development stage, you need to understand the overall risks facing the project and how these risks should be allocated. The project team should consider the following:

- How mature is the project team?

- What is the overall value of the risks?

- Which risks is the project team going to allocate to the suppliers?

- What risks register are we going to include in the tender package to get the view of the suppliers?

- What type of contract is suitable for the package to reflect the risk allocation?

- How can we refine our selection criteria to reflect the risk behaviour and culture we intend to see on the project?

Delivery Phase

At this phase, the ability to influence risk is minimal; it is mainly about mitigating and controlling risk. At this phase, the delivery team should be doing the following:

- Risk should be transparent, and everyone on the team should be aware of the risks that are being controlled, including the gangs at the work front.

- What additional risks are being introduced and need to be shared with the team and controlled?

Throughout the various stages, risks should be at the forefront of the team's mind. The team must understand how the decisions being made at that stage affect the risk profile for the next stage and what other risks their decisions introduce in the next stage.

Create a Useful Risk Register

What is a Project Risk?

Project risk is defined by the Project Management Institute as 'an uncertain event or condition that, if it occurs, has a positive or negative effect on a project's objectives'.

The Association of Project Managers defines a risk event as 'an uncertain event or set of circumstances that would, if it occurred, have an effect on the achievement of one or more objectives' — APM Body of Knowledge 6th Edition

According to **ISO** 31000, **risk** is the 'effect of uncertainty on objectives', and an 'effect' is a positive or negative deviation from what is expected.

Two of the definitions are clear on the fact that a risk may have a negative or positive effect. Note that the APM definition does not state what type of effect the risk may have on the project. A negative risk will be seen as a threat, and a positive risk will be seen as an opportunity.

In effect, a risk is anything that can cause an impact — either negative or positive — on schedule, cost, or performance. A risk won't have a 100% probability of occurring. Anything with a 100% probability of occurring is a problem, not a risk. A problem is a negative consequence with a certain, or almost certain, probability of occurrence. If something is a problem, then you need to start looking at corrective action rather than treating it as a risk.

Some Risk Identification Pitfalls

Sometimes during risk identification, we tend to include our own 'worries' in the risk register rather than what the project risks are. 'Worries' are small-scale, routine, day-to-day uncertainties that standard project procedures should address. For example, should 'Design not approved by Category 3 checker' really be on the risk register? We go through the process of selecting a competent designer who then bases their design on codes of practice, which is then checked by an independent team to ensure the design is right. Is it really a risk that the design won't be accepted, or it is just a 'worry'? Another example of risk that is prevalent in the industry is 'inaccurate or incomplete specifications'. The standard project process will include the authors, reviewers, and approver, and, so, should this really be in the project risk register? One can refer to these 'worries' as 'business-as-usual risks'.

Another type of risk that sometimes appears on risk registers, which may not bode well for the project manager, is 'failure to estimate the costs accurately'. Most projects will have 'estimating uncertainty (EU)' included in the budget for that stage of the project. To, therefore, include such a risk gives the impression of doubling up on risk. Is this really a risk, or you are uncertain that you've estimated the work properly and you're trying to double up?

When 'worries' and 'issues/problems' are captured on a risk register, it gives the impression that the risk register is a get-out-of-jail plan for when problems start to occur or an explanation of why the budget is running over. You should make sure that the project has not been approved on minimal costs just to get it through the approval process even though there are 'issues' that are known and should have been captured in the baseline cost.

Identifying Risks Effectively

It is critical that risk identification starts at the concept stage of the project. At the concept stage, identification of the sources of risk is more critical than the individual risks themselves.

Risk identification should be undertaken at each stage of the project lifecycle and should be very rigorous, with the right expertise and team involved in the identification. The following are some of the ways to ensure that the right risks are being identified and recorded:

- Using lessons learnt from other projects in general and also from similar projects.

- Brainstorming. To ensure that the brainstorming is effective, you need to assemble a team which consists of people of different technical backgrounds, cultures, and industries to reap the maximum benefit. The scene should be set to identify both opportunities and threats. Most people are tuned, when they hear the word 'risk', to start identifying only the negative impacts. The project manager should be clear at the onset to encourage the team to consider both threats and opportunities.

- Reviewing whether the assumptions that the project-development stage was based on introduce risks to the project.

- Reviewing what risk each stage of the project may have introduced.

- Reviewing the constraints on the project to understand the risks these constraints introduce to the project. You need to consider whether the critical threats can be removed by changing the project constraints or whether opportunities can be exploited by tweaking the constraints.

- SWOT Analysis. Identifying the strengths, weakness, opportunities, and threats of the project.

- Scheduling deep dives. Undertaking programme/schedule deep dives will uncover risks you may not have considered.

- Undertaking constructability reviews will uncover risks that you have not considered and better ways of undertaking the project to save money and shave time off the schedule.

- Involving the operations team in the risk-identification exercise.

A good risk description will have the event, the cause, and the consequence. Also, the statement should be concise and quantitative, captures the consequence in the statement, and uses an 'If then' format. It should answer the following questions:

- What could happen?

- Why could it happen?

- Why do we care?

All risk identified should be recorded on a risk register and be given owners. Risk owners should be people who are best placed to address that risk.

You will need to test whether you have recorded the right risks on the register. One way of doing this is by asking suppliers and team members at different levels what is keeping them awake at night. The risks they identify should be on your register, or you should have a strong reason why they are not.

A risk register is an important tool, but more often than not, it becomes a box-ticking exercise for project leaders to show their seniors that they are doing their job.

Assessing the Risks Effectively

How significant is each risk in terms of its probability of occurrence and its impact should it occur? In assessing the risk, you need to be able to answer the following questions:

- What can go wrong?

- What is the frequency of this occurring?

- What are the consequences if it occurs?

Although risk assessment is thought to be either quantitative or qualitative, whichever method you choose, risk assessment is always subjective. One person's perception of the severity and characteristics of a particular risk will differ from that of another.

If we knew the exact probability of a risk occurring and its exact consequence, then it wouldn't be a risk. The probability of something occurring — whether 10%, 20%, 30%, etc., will always be subjective. Its consequence will also have some amount of subjectivity, but consequences can be predicted a bit better than the probability of it occurring. For example, the probability of an interfacing project delivering the power supply for your project could be predicted by how well they are performing on their project. You can't be accurate on the probability, but you may be close, which may be good enough. The consequence may be hiring a generator whose cost can be predicted closely enough. In other circumstances, the impact may be on schedule. Without knowing the exact size of the risk, the exact impact on the schedule may be the best guess. However, by understanding the project prelims and other costs, you can translate that schedule impact into costs.

There are other risks, like ground conditions, for which your prediction may not follow the route as described above. Some risks may be easier to assess than others and may involve varying degrees of subjectivity. To help in reducing the subjectivity in assessing the risks, the following can be employed:

- Test the assumptions of the risk assessment. Do they mirror reality?

- Use expert opinion.

- What does historical data indicate?

- Are there any lessons learnt that you could use to base this on?

- Brainstorm with other experts.

- Use ranges of probability.

Some organisations will multiply the probability and consequence to achieve an expected value for the risk and sum all of these up to arrive at a risk pot. Others prefer using a Monte Carlo Analysis to arrive at a risk exposure. A contingency of P50 at a PM level, P90 at project senior leadership level and P95 at client's level.

A Monte Carlo Analysis can give you an idea of the contingency you need overall for the project. The expected value will help you in decision-making if the cost of a mitigation plan is worth it. Both should be used on the project.

Developing Effective Risk Mitigation Plans

Risks are better averted at the early stages of the project lifecycle, where decisions you make influence the risks you introduce in the project. This is the reason we recommend treating risk management as part of the lifecycle process of the project. If you leave the risk to the later stages, you tend to be left with just controlling the risk and reducing the impact of the risk. The risk-mitigation plans that are developed for each individual risk need to have an effect on the risk that it is mitigating unless you have decided to accept the risk and do nothing about it. Some projects risk-mitigation plans turn into simply another meeting which does nothing to reduce the probability of the risk occurring or reducing the impact if it occurs. The following can be helpful in developing effective mitigation plans for the individual risk:

1. Undertake a root-cause analysis to understand how the risk was introduced.

a. Was this due to a design decision? Can the basis of the design be changed to reduce the probability of the risk occurring or its impact? An example would be the use of pad foundation in contaminated ground, which could result in substantial costs. One may opt for a different form of piles to reduce the cost of the contaminated ground being excavated and disposed of.

b. Was this risk introduced by an additional scope that can be removed from the project? Can the scope of the work be modified?

c. Is the risk being introduced due to how the project was split into packages — that is, is it an interface risk? Can the package be redefined to remove the risk?

d. Is the risk being introduced due to the type of conditions of the contract being recommended for the package?

e. Is the risk being introduced due to the relationship with significant stakeholders, like the environmental agency, the council, or other government agencies?

f. Is a major stakeholder best placed to undertake the work to remove the risk? For example, in the United Kingdom, projects like the HS2 will have significant interfaces with Network Rail (UK rail operator). In some cases, allowing Network Rail to deliver those packages may remove the risk.

2. Be aware of the risks that your mitigation plans may introduce. You may transfer a scope to a stakeholder to remove a particular risk but introduce a risk of the stakeholder meeting your timescales. You need to weigh the

risk you have avoided and what you are introducing to ensure you are making the right decision.

3. Use lessons learnt from other projects to understand if there are better ways of mitigating the risks.

4. Don't do it alone. Use a team of experts to undertake the root-cause analysis.

5. Use the supplier's experience to test your mitigation plans.

6. Develop a contingency breakage plan on how you will release a contingency whose risk has truly passed.

Don't Forget Opportunities

Remember that risks consist of both threats and opportunities. Identification of risks is, therefore, identification of both threats and opportunities. It is often the case that people are focused on all the things that could go wrong on a project but fail to identify situations that could be exploited to benefit the project. Focusing only on threats can sometimes demotivate a team. Focusing on opportunities will lift the team and motivate the team towards the collective goals.

Your goal here is to identify as many opportunities as threats. I am not saying, 'Limit the risks you identify'. However, there needs to be a conscious effort to find opportunities that can be exploited to better the project.

Identifying opportunities involves the following:

- **Challenging the design basis**

    Often, very scarce information is available during the Business Case stage, which causes a pessimistic point of view in creating the premises of the design deliverables. As the project moves through its various phases, more knowledge is gained, and it becomes possible to challenge the original design assumptions, saving the project money.

- **Promoting new ways of working**

  Some industries get stuck in ways of working which sometimes are not efficient. It is the 'This is what we have always done' mentality. Learning from other industries and doing things slightly different may create an opportunity for saving time and cost. For example, in the United Kingdom, the Rail industry takes rail possessions to complete a critical piece of work within a short window. These possessions can sometimes be expensive, but they do save time on the railway and, in effect, save money in the long run. At times, it may not be the most efficient way for the government overall. The Highway industry will also put on traffic managements that will go on for months on end, which may save money for the project but not for the country's economy. In the Nuclear industry, similar work done in another industry may cost tons of money because of a blanket safety case which invokes a certain method of working that is sometimes not even required if you review the reasons in more detail. There is no right or wrong way, as every project goal will determine what method of working is best for it. The point I am making here is not to be afraid to borrow from other industries and not to be limited by what the norm is in that industry.

- **Introducing innovative solutions**

  This overlaps a bit with my previous points. There are solutions that are completely novel and others that are novel only to that particular industry. Some examples: We introduced ScrewFast micropiles into the Highway industry for technology projects and had to go through a departure process to allow us to use it for the first time. This saved us significant time and money. However, the ScrewFast micropiles were being used in the Rail industry. In a similar vein, to use Reco wall in the Rail industry to save money on a project, we had to apply for a departure to make it possible. However, this solution was already being used in the Highway industry. Fibre-reinforced tunnel segments are currently not used in safety-classified nuclear structures in the United Kingdom. However, this is a common practice in other sectors. There is also innovation which involves using solutions already established in other countries. The project manager should consider all of these to save cost and time on their projects. However, note that to develop true innovation, senior leaders should understand that project leaders will occasionally get it wrong. Punishing project leaders on an effort in innovation is a sure way of extinguishing any further efforts in that direction.

- **Adopting supplier procedures**

  At times, the supplier's procedures for certain items of work may be better than the client's. Adopting these could save the project a significant amount of money.

- **Root-cause analysis of threats**

  Root-cause analysis of threats may identify opportunities to improve the schedule, save money, improve quality, and create a better working environment for the project.

Understand the Different Types of Risk Registers on Projects

Sometimes it gets a bit confusing with the various risk registers on a construction project. There is the client's risk register, the supplier's risk register, the health and safety risk register, and the risk register that some contracts like the NEC ECC contracts refer to. How do all these risk registers relate?

The health and safety risk register records risks with the likelihood that a person may be harmed or suffer adverse health effects if exposed to a hazard. These risks need to be rigorously identified and controlled; they may have a significant financial impact. But this is not the risk register that we are referring to in this section.

The first risk register that will be developed after the chosen option in a Business Case on a project is what I will call the project risk register, which the client's project manager will develop. The risks on this register, together with the project estimates and estimating uncertainty, will form the project's budget.

After a client decides to construct the work, they will first decide how they want to share or allocate risk, depending on the maturity of their design/scope or their risk appetite. This determines the type of contract they choose and the form of relationship they want to have with their supplier. Therefore, the choice of contract is a huge risk-allocation work that you cannot take lightly. These days, the NEC ECC form of contract is becoming widely used on infrastructure projects in the United Kingdom, and, even with that, there are several options regarding risk allocation.

After the client chooses a form of contract and allocates the risks, their risk register will still make allowance for the risk they have transferred to the supplier. The supplier will have their own risk register to help them control risks that are their contractual responsibility. The client pays a premium for these risks that they have transferred, but, depending on the contract, they may still be liable for the risks when they occur. I use the word 'may' because, in target-cost contracts, the client will still be liable for some of the effects of the risks when they occur. This is very important for the client to know. It will determine their attitude toward risk control and help them to determine what they believe to be the contractor's risk.

Regardless of whose contractual responsibility a risk is, the client is likely to bear the overall reputational damage when risks occur. Due to this, some collaborative forms of contract like the NEC ECC have what is called the Risk Register. Other forms of contract may not have this formal requirement for a risk register. But any client wanting to develop a collaborative relationship with their supplier will have a joint risk register. This risk register is a means for the two parties to work collaboratively to control the risks on the project. The value and accountability for the risks on this risk register is determined by the contract.

So invariably, you are likely to have the following risk registers on a project:

1. **Health and Safety Risk Register.** This addresses risks that will cause harm to humans. These are mainly CDM risks, and, although this risk register will have a significant financial impact, it is not the risk register that is referred to when discussing budget.
2. **Project Risk Register.** This consists of the overall project risks and forms part of the budget for the project.
3. **Supplier Risk Register.** This is a register you may not normally see. It lists all the risks that the contract identifies as the contractor's risk and other risks that the contractor believes they need to control to protect their margins.

The supplier will normally consider the value of this in their bid for the work.

4. **NEC ECC Risk Register or a Joint Risk Register.** This is a register that either the contract requires or both parties decide they will use collaboratively to control risks on the project. The value and accountability of these risks are determined by the contract.

Note that certain risks will be on the Project Risk Register that will not necessarily be on the joint risk register or the NEC ECC Risk Register, as they cannot be controlled by the contract; therefore, the client controls this separately.

One of the fears that the client's team have always harboured about having a joint risk register is that, if the supplier knows the value we have allocated to that risk, then they will create situations to make use of that budget. Now I won't say these are not well-founded fears, but what I will say is that this goes back to how much trust you have with each party. Alternatively, the client need not disclose what they have allowed for those risks. The most important thing is controlling the risk efficiently. Certain risk mitigations require expending money to either remove the threat or increase the chances of the opportunity occurring. Trust is built in a relationship, and, if the client is not comfortable in disclosing how much they have allowed, they can still decide after the supplier has submitted the cost of the mitigation.

On the other hand, the supplier may have a risk brewing, and if they are working hard to control it, they may be reluctant to let the client know. I have encountered several of these risk situations which sometimes became too late to address, or I luckily found out through a good relationship with the main supplier's team member. Such risks obviously should be on the joint risk register. However, some leads of suppliers may claim it is their risk, that they are working to control it, and that there was no need to inform the client. All risks will impact the client one way or the other when they occur, so it is best if they are communicated to the client. All of these issues boil down to the relationship between the client and the supplier and how the client has treated certain situations in the past. Building a strong collaborative relationship with your suppliers is, therefore, an overall critical risk-mitigation measure.

Make Risk Management the Basis of Your Decision-Making Process

In conclusion, risk management, when undertaken properly, will help save a project from going into crisis. This should also be treated as a project-lifecycle activity and be the basis of decision-making on the project. Every decision you make on a project will either introduce a new risk, remove a risk, or mitigate a risk. Decisions should always be made on a project by asking yourself the following:

1. What new risk am I introducing?
2. What risk am I removing?
3. What risk am I mitigating?

The project team should have a culture of asking themselves these three questions whenever they are making decisions. This should include everyone — from designers, contractors installing the physical work, project managers, stakeholders, and everyone who is working on the project. Although specific risks will be allocated to parties who are best able to manage the risk, risk management on a project is everyone's job. Everyone on a project makes a decision one way or the other and, therefore, affects the risks of a project. Due to this, the following will be helpful to ensure that risk management is effective on the project:

• Make risk management everyone's business on the project.

- Decision-making on the project should take into account their effect on the risk profile.

- Major risks and their mitigation measures should be regularly discussed at project meetings and not just at-risk meetings.

- Risk ownership and the impact if the risk occurs should be transparent throughout the project.

- Risk-mitigation measures should be broken down to a level where men on the work front can apply and form part of their work discussion if appropriate.

- Escalation routes of risks should be well defined and communicated and also trigger points predefined.

- A risk-mature senior team that encourages team members to alert them when risks are likely to occur and not resort to a blame culture.

- Risk meetings should be used to find solutions and assess the landscape and not used as a box-ticking exercise.

Chapter 8:

Reactive Troubleshooting

'Life is 10% what happens to you and 90% how you react to it.' — *Charles R. Swindoll*

In dealing with risk management, we are dealing with the known unknowns; in troubleshooting, we are dealing with some known unknowns that weren't properly controlled and had caused the project to go into crisis and unknown unknowns.

I really don't like the word 'problem' used in any form and have tried to change my vocabulary to 'challenge' instead. Because to me, every challenge develops us. However, in this section of the book, I will use the word 'problem' as it fits certain defined descriptions that the industries use in 'troubleshooting'.

Most project leaders assume that once a project is properly planned and you identify risks using all the proactive measures, then you will never have a problem. This can be true of small, non-complex projects but not so for large infrastructure projects, which tend to be complex. Some stakeholders also assume that once there is a problem on a project, then the project manager and the team managing it are at fault and need to be replaced. The belief is that risk can be anticipated and projects executed as planned.

Proactive risk management and reactive troubleshooting in project management are similar to how we deal with fire in fire management. The world of fire management has come a long way, with fire standards, codes of practice, and equipment installed in buildings — and yet we have firefighters. No one says that we do not need firefighters because we have great standards and codes to prevent fires from starting. Proactive risk management is similar to prevention programmes in fire management, with reactive troubleshooting the equivalent of firefighters. This is because one cannot provide for all the contingencies that could occur on a project, as that is not practical.

Large infrastructure projects with many stakeholders are like complex systems and are sometimes unpredictable since they entail unforeseen risks and events that cannot be predicted. Given the impracticability of pre-planning for every possible contingency, large infrastructure projects will face problems in their life cycle. The goal is to limit the number of these problems and salvage them when they do happen.

To deliver large infrastructure projects successfully, one needs a combination of proactive risk management and reactive troubleshooting skills in order to be successful.

'Troubleshooting', according to The Cambridge Dictionary, is 'discovering why something does not work effectively and making suggestions about how to improve it'.

Project troubleshooting is, therefore, 'discovering why a project is significantly outside its agreed tolerances, finding solutions to these discovered reasons, and implementing them successfully'. Project troubleshooting applies problem-solving techniques to projects.

We read a lot about troubleshooting our gadgets when they malfunction. However, 'project troubleshooting' is rarely mentioned in project-management courses. Most project managers who have become good at troubleshooting happened to firefight several times and picked up some excellent skills whilst they went through the issues. The same process for troubleshooting malfunctioning gadgets can be applied to projects.

Large infrastructure projects are normally run by experienced project managers, and the reasons they sometimes go into crisis are more complex than what is normally identified as causes of project failures. There are many reasons why projects go into crisis, but the main ones are:

- Stakeholders and clients want more than they are prepared to pay for the project. This sometimes causes underestimating the real price of the project just to gain approval or make the Business Case attractive. The thinking here is, 'We will find some way to cut other costs later'.

- Clients normally do not involve the tier 1 & 2 contractors when producing the costs estimates for the Business Case. This results in underestimating the project from the outset.

- With respect to work packages, clients sometimes feel contractors are charity organisations and want to increase their scope without a corresponding increase in price. The procurement models cause contractors to under-price, and the project starts with a claim mentality, which makes the relationship go sour. A bad relationship between a client and their contractor is a recipe for a project to go into crisis.

- The objectives and goals of a project are normally not very clear at the initiation stage of a project. Schedule and cost estimates for the project tend, therefore, not to be accurate.

- Political pressure on large infrastructure projects is very high. Some of these projects are political ideas, and, therefore, they are on a tight budget due to intense public pressure. The government, therefore, may over-promise but under-deliver.

- Client leadership is sometimes a master-servant relationship with their suppliers. This relationship does not provide the right leadership or the high-performance environment required to meet the changing needs of a complex project.

- Lack of a coherent vision from the senior leadership team.

- Different understanding of what success looks like. This can occur between the various stakeholders or even between the client and their suppliers.

- The unknown risks of a project occurring.

- Poor scope management and not monitoring, controlling, and updating the schedule.

- Team members are not clear of what is required of them nor the goals of the project. They are also not empowered nor do they see themselves as part of the team.

- Improper control of quality.

- Not the right type of resources (e.g. technology).

- Processes and procedures not tailored to the project.

First, one needs to understand whether the project is really in trouble or whether it is simply perceived to be in trouble. Is the project completely out of the agreed tolerances? At times a project may be in trouble; however, the project manager may have already put a recovery plan in place which may be working and therefore just requires monitoring.

After a project has been identified as 'in trouble', the recovering of the project should be treated as a project in itself. Therefore, the troubleshooter should do the following:

- Agree what success will look like

- Agree on the timescales for the recovery phase

- Agree on resources needed for the recovery

- Agree on how the recovery plan will be monitored

One should never assume the cause for a project being in crisis. An in-depth search for the cause should be conducted. With some projects, once the cause of the problem is identified, the solution seems obvious. In some cases, there can be several solutions. You need to review all of the solutions in order to arrive at the best solution for the identified cause of the problem.

Troubleshooting a project should follow the below seven steps:

1. Present state — Understanding and being clear about the current state of the project
2. Goal state — Understanding where you want to be or what you want to achieve
3. Conduct a disciplined search for the causes of your present stage
4. Conduct a disciplined search for all solutions
5. Select the most suitable solutions

6. Implement the solutions

7. Monitor the effectiveness of the solution selected

Searching for the Causes of Your Present State

Problems can be either well-defined or ill-defined. With a well-defined problem, the project leader will direct all their resources towards finding a solution, whereas in an ill-defined problem, resources will be directed first towards defining the problem. However, for a complex infrastructure project, what you see on the surface may not be the reason for the crisis. Therefore, the project leader should not jump immediately into solution mode but rigorously search for the underlining causes of why the project is in crisis. In most cases, there will be several reasons why a project is in crisis, and, therefore, there may be several solutions.

The following are ways of identifying the cause of a crisis:

- Interview individual members of the project team to understand their perspective on what is being done or not being done. This should include suppliers, team members, and other stakeholders.

- Check whether standard project-management processes are being implemented. Investigate the following areas:

  » People and supplier relationships

  » Leadership behaviours

  » Project controls procedures

  » Commercial management and procurement procedures

  » Construction procedures

  » Design processes

> » Risk-management processes and how the team approaches this
>
> » Quality-management processes
>
> » Stakeholder management
>
> » Communication processes
>
> » People's understanding of their specific roles for the project
>
> » How lessons are learnt and captured

- Use the outcomes of the investigations and interviews to conduct a fishbone analysis or use 5 Whys to understand the causes of the identified issues. There may be reasons for people behaving the way they are or for not using certain processes. It may be a lack of training, procedures not being communicated, or not having the right skills. Do not settle for the surface causes; you need to delve deeper to understand the root causes.

Searching for Solutions

Once the problems are properly defined and the causes understood, the solutions are normally obvious. However, one needs to select the best solutions for the issues encountered. The following are ways to identify solutions:

- Brainstorming — Use a small group of people, not more than 7 in number, to come up with a large number of ideas, and develop them until you have an optimal solution.

- Research — There is no new problem under the sun. Someone has had a similar issue and has addressed it before. Research it on the Internet and adapt existing solutions to similar problems.

- Sometimes the project manager has been shaped by the issues of the problem and will find it difficult to think outside the box. It is sometimes helpful to bring a team with a fresh pair of eyes to think outside the box and come up with creative solutions. This is what is called a 'tiger team'.

Implementation and Monitoring of the Solutions

Once the appropriate solutions have been selected, they need to be implemented immediately. Some of these may require changes in the way of working, and you may require change agents in the team to help adopt the change. Consider the steps of JP Kotter's *Leading Change* to implement your changes.

It is very important you gain buy-in from the team that will be implementing the change. This will be easier if the project leader and some team members are involved in the troubleshooting process or at least feel empowered. Dates should be set for when the changes will be completely implemented and for when benefits of the changes will be realised.

A team should be set up to review the progress of the changes and tweak them if required.

Obstacles to Problem Solving

Whilst searching for the underlying problems, one needs to be cognisant of the following obstacles to problem-solving and how to get around them:

- Politics — When troubleshooting is conducted by an outside team other than the current team running the project, the project team sometimes may be resistant to the outside team and try to be obstructive. They may feel that they are being blamed for not managing the project properly. A lot of skill will be required to assure the project team that the outside team is there to help. This is easier if the project leader is allowed to be one of the major stakeholders in the troubleshooting team and made to feel they are part of the troubleshooting.

- Confirmation Bias — The human mind sometimes will come to conclusions about an issue and then search for evidence to confirm that conclusion and reject any evidence which goes against what it has already concluded are the facts. We get into a cycle of gathering evidence to support our own beliefs and then pointing to the evidence gathered specifically to confirm the belief as the reason for the belief. Everyone is susceptible to confirmation bias, and this can occur whilst troubleshooting projects. You can, therefore, arrive at causes for crisis on a project which are not actually the causes but your own limits shaped by your own experiences or environment.

To avoid confirmation bias, you need to surround yourself with a diverse group of people who are confident enough to challenge your views. You need to go out of your way to search for opposing evidence to your conclusions. It is also important to have someone you respect play 'devil's advocate' for your final conclusions.

You also need to consider your 'thinking preference'. If you are someone who, like me, is wholly optimistic, you may need to put a pessimistic hat on and consider the evidence from another viewpoint — and vice versa if you are a pessimist.

You can also employ 'Six Thinking Hats', created by Edward de Bono and published in his 1985 book to prevent confirmation bias.

In troubleshooting a project, it is best to put together a team of different backgrounds and expertise who will assess the situation from different points of view.

- Mental set — Abraham Luchins discovered that people have an inclination to attempt to solve problems in a manner that has proved successful in their previous experience, even if there are more efficient and simpler ways. In many cases, experience can allow us to quickly troubleshoot a crisis on projects and save time and money. However, in some instances, past experience can also block us from identifying more efficient solutions to the crisis.

  In troubleshooting projects, to ensure you have considered the best solutions, it is sometimes good to have some less-experienced, but innovative team members, who may come up with solutions that experienced people's mental sets may be preventing them from capturing.

- Unnecessary constraints — When defining the scope of the troubleshooting work, try not to set unnecessary constraints which make it difficult to find the right solution. Unnecessary constraints can also result from over-reliance on past experience to come up with a solution, without thinking outside the box.

- Irrelevant information — Since troubleshooting will involve interviewing people and gathering information to understand the causes of the project crisis, people will give you information that may not be relevant to the cause of the crisis. You need to understand the goal of the work and the motives of the people being interviewed.

Tiger Teams

A 1964 paper defined a tiger team as 'a team of undomesticated and uninhibited technical specialists, selected for their experience, energy, and imagination, and assigned to track down relentlessly every possible source of failure in a spacecraft subsystem'.

A tiger team consists of high-performing team members with exceptional communication, meeting, work-process, and leadership skills. These team members have high-level listening skills and consist of people who are team players and can suppress their own egos for the benefit of the team. On large infrastructure projects, it pays when some members of the tiger team have Lean or Six Sigma competencies. Members should be people who can submit to authority and also take authority when required. The people making up the tiger team should be skilled in implementing change. They should also be very well read and have high levels of emotional intelligence, as they will need to be able to understand different people's perspectives on the issues of the project.

According to Lencioni (2002), an effective troubleshooting team exhibits the following five characteristics:

- **Trust and respect:** The team functions as a unit; members feel free to say what they think without the threat of repercussions from organisational politics.

- **Uninhibited constructive conflict:** Total focus on content and ideas.

- **Commitment:** Every team member participates, with no observers, and everyone contributes.

- **Accountability:** Members hold each other accountable for results; this promotes a slacker-free environment.

- **Common goals:** Members place common goals above individual needs.

Troubleshooting, just like proactive risk management, is a critical aspect of managing large infrastructure projects as problems *will* come up in these types of projects; it is just a matter of when. Preparation will improve your chances for success in solving them. Large Infrastructure projects should, therefore, always ensure that their project managers are equipped with troubleshooting skills.

Note that solutions to significant crisis on projects take time to take effect. Senior leadership, therefore, need to give adequate time for this. Too often results are expected quickly. When recovery is slower than expected, a new plan is often adopted when there was nothing wrong with the first.

Chapter 9:

Supplier Collaboration

Collaboration is a hot topic on every project these days. We were once asked by a supplier during the tender phase whether we wanted to enter into a 'collaborative relationship' or a 'truly collaborative relationship'. The 'truly collaborative relationship' when we enquired was a higher price!

I have held workshops for project teams where I have mentioned that we need to form a collaborative partnership to be high-performing on the project. I normally will hear a few statements which raise alarm bells on whether people really understand what collaboration is. Some will say, 'We need to work in a way that the contract is put in the drawer and never looked at'. I, for one, don't believe a project manager should run a project without understanding what is in the contract. How will you know what is required to be delivered if you don't know what is in the contract? How will you monitor the project and prevent it from going into crisis if you are not following the processes? I will sometimes also hear statements like 'Collaboration is not easy'. Yes, we all know that; living with your spouse is not easy, either. Halfway through the workshop, the contractor may say, 'If I put my contract hat on'. Yes — we never asked you to take it off. That would be unfair because we want you to deliver our scope in the agreed time with the right quality'. The word 'collaboration' is bandied about a lot; however, most people really do not understand what it means or what it takes.

The best book I have read on collaboration is Collaborative Leadership, by David Archer and Alex Cameron. I recommend that every project leader read this book. This book discusses forming collaborative relationships in general and how leaders in a collaborative relationship should conduct themselves. The book gives several tools that are applicable across all projects and great examples from industry leaders. In this book, however, our focus will be on how collaboration should be applied in delivering large infrastructure projects.

Large infrastructure projects are normally complex and are subject to change; therefore, supplier collaboration is key to its success. As a matter of fact, I do not believe a large infrastructure project can be successful without collaborating effectively with your suppliers. It is really your only way to ensure that your project goals are achieved.

What is Collaboration?

Business dictionaries define 'collaboration' as 'a cooperative arrangement in which two or more parties (which may or may not have any previous relationship) work jointly towards a common goal'. If one takes into consideration this definition, then all clients are in some form of a collaborative relationship with their suppliers. Therefore, the question of whether you are going to be in a collaborative relationship or not is a moot point. Once you take a supplier on board to deliver a project, you should be working towards the same goals of delivering the project on budget and on time. The reasons behind achieving these goals may be different. The supplier's reasons may be to make a profit and improve their image in the industry, and the client's reasons may be as per their Business Case. However, on the project, you should be working to achieve the same goal. So, in a

144

sense, you are in a collaborative relationship when you get a supplier on board to construct an infrastructure project.

When people say, 'We need to collaborate on infrastructure projects', what they mean is, 'We need to increase the amount of collaboration in the relationship'. This is very important to understand, as it clarifies the discussion on whether we collaborate with our suppliers or not. Also, note that collaboration is not just saying yes to everything!

Collaborative Working

Collaborative working in the industry is used to refer to various ways in which two or more organisations decide to work together. This will range from informal networking through joint deliveries to a full merger.

In the construction industry, collaborative working may take the following forms:

- Delivery Partners relationships. In these cases, the delivery partners support the clients in managing the project; however, they are not the ones constructing the work themselves.

- Alliance between the client and suppliers. This is where there is a joint management team to undertake the work. Network Rail in the UK has been successful in using this to deliver a number of their projects, including the Hitching Viaduct. Network Rail also has a number of alliances with the train operators, for example, South West Trains.;

- Joint ventures between two or more suppliers to undertake work that just one of the suppliers may not have the capability for. This is common on very large construction projects like Hinkley Point C, High Speed 2, and Cross

Rail in the United Kingdom, where two suppliers form a partnership to construct the infrastructure work. Some of these joint ventures may keep their individual names, and others will register a new company name to deliver the package of work.

- Standard Client — Supplier contract arrangement with an agreed way of working which is documented and the processes followed. The collaborative working document may be in the form of the BS11000 Relationship Management document.

- Some forms of contracts, like the NEC ECC, encourage collaborative working. Clause 10.1 of this contract starts with promoting this form of working. The risk-reduction clause 16 is also intended to increase the collaboration in the relationship. The target-cost options are mainly driving towards high levels of collaboration in the relationship.

- Other forms of client-supplier contracts, like the JCT, ICE, etc. These contracts on their own have very low levels of collaboration in the relationship. They are more transactional in nature.

For the purposes of this book, our focus is on the relationship between the client body and the supplier responsible for constructing the work — not the delivery partner who becomes part of the client organisation. In very non-complex, straight-forward projects, you may get away with a standard old form of contract and treat it in a transactional manner, with low levels of collaboration, and still succeed. However, as the project increases in size and complexity, your chances of being successful increases, as the level of collaboration in the relationship also increases.

Some of the benefits of high levels of collaborative working in the relationship between the client and supplier in large infrastructure projects are:

- A greater focus on solving challenges

- Fewer surprises for either party

- A more united front and greater energy in the team

- Financial savings and better use of resources

- Best practice and information sharing which the client can transfer to their other packages/projects

- Greater flexibility to accommodate changes in the project

- Better communication across the project

- Greater energy to seek out threats and address them

- Greater energy to identify opportunities for the project

Choosing the Right Collaboration for Your Project

There are many benefits for a project with high levels of collaborative working; however, there are challenges in achieving high levels of collaboration which make it resource intensive. Some of the issues you may come across or may need to overcome are:

- Depending on the level of collaboration you opt for, decision making may become more complex. Unilateral decision making by the client on the contract will not bode well for the collaboration relationship.

- Personalities who are entrenched in transactional relationships. These may be very senior people who are used

147

to working with the old forms of contract and are used to the claim mentality of old forms of contract and the reputation some suppliers have gained.

- Lack of experience in the team for working on projects with high levels of collaboration.

- Trying to overcome the different organisational cultures.

- Loss of clarity on roles and responsibilities.

The above challenges are resource intensive to address. This means that one needs to be careful about the levels of collaboration for the project. The levels of collaboration you choose should be commensurate with the benefits that you will obtain from the contract.

What Level of Collaboration do you need?

There are two main forms of collaboration between the client and supplier in the construction industry — a client-supplier transactional relationship at one end and an alliance between the client and the supplier on the other end. For most infrastructure projects, collaboration falls somewhere between these two. The confusion arises when the leaders do not define where they sit at the onset of the collaboration spectrum, which then leads to confusion for the various teams. This also causes people to feel used when the other party does not put in the same effort. The more complex a project is, the higher the levels of collaboration required to ensure its success.

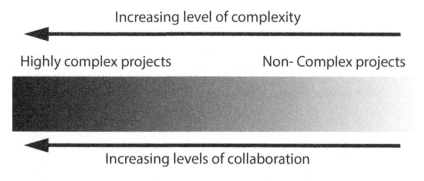

Increasing level of complexity

Highly complex projects   Non- Complex projects

Increasing levels of collaboration

Partnership (example Alliance or better)
- Select supplier on culture and technical fit not cost
- Develop charter
- Aligned objectives and goals
- Colocation of team
- Team approach to risk management
- Joint Project Leadership team
- Drive towards one team mentality
- Consider adoption of Lean Construction

Client – supplier transactional relationship.
- Sign the contract
- Leave the contractor to do their work
- Monitor milestones
- Make payments

Figure 9.1 Complexity and collaboration levels spectrum

Large infrastructure projects are complex and generally require large levels of collaboration to make them successful. However, the complexity of a large infrastructure project is such that although one package in the project may require large levels of collaboration to be successful, another may be better suited to a simple transactional relationship. An example is a large Nuclear project. This involves several specialist plants as well as the civil infrastructure construction. It may be necessary to deliver one particular package using a straightforward transactional relationship and another using high levels of collaboration.

So, considering the challenges you will face in using high levels of collaboration, you need to determine from the outset what levels of collaboration are beneficial for the project or package. The client can enter into several collaborative relationships with the suppliers they work with on the same large infrastructure project; it is not a one size fits all. This is because different packages on the same large infrastructure project may require a different collaborative approach.

The following are some of the things you need to consider on the level of collaboration you need for the project or package of work:

- Is the project completely defined, with changes unlikely to occur? If this is the case, you may want to leave the supplier constructing the work to get on with it. Low levels of collaboration may be OK.

- Does the project have several interfaces, and are the interfaces likely to affect each package? If the answer is 'Yes', you will need high levels of collaboration.

- What is the client's expertise in this aspect of work? For example, Network Rail in the UK normally has team members with more experience in blockade and track-replacement work than most suppliers, and, therefore, leaving a supplier by themselves may not be the right decision. A higher level of collaboration may be required to make the project successful.

- Past experience with the supplier. Is it better to start from low levels of collaboration until each gains the trust of the other?

- What are the structures required to be in place for the collaborative relationship to be successful? What level of collaboration will make the implementation of these structures worthwhile?

- Does the project involve several interactions with legislative bodies like the Environmental Agency, ONR, HSE, etc.? If that is the case then you may need very high levels of collaboration, as the clients may be better equipped to interact with these organisations.

The supplier and client team will have to agree on the level of collaboration they believe is appropriate for undertaking the project. It is important to document your ways of working and how you will tackle problems and escalate issues. Expectations of each partner will need to be documented. The BS11000 Relationship Management template provides a framework for documenting your ways of working, expectations, and how you will deal with issues.

The Pillars of Successful Collaboration for Complex Infrastructure Projects

The reasons people shy away from collaboration is that they feel one party wants to take advantage of the other in the guise of collaboration. This is why clients' employees will state that collaboration is not easy, and the supplier will say, 'When I put my contractual hat on'. For collaboration to be successful in the construction of a complex infrastructure project, there are certain pillars that should be in place:

1. Robust Contract
2. Right behaviours
3. A strong collaborative leadership

A Robust Contract

Putting the contract in the drawer and pretending you are in a collaborative relationship is not going to help anyone. The contract determines the scope of work and what is required of the supplier and client; it determines the governance that everyone should follow, and it is what gives each party confidence that the other will fulfil their responsibilities. This does not mean that the client should stick to processes in the contract which don't work if the supplier's processes are a better fit for the job. This does not mean you throw the contract requirements away either. What you do is by agreement — you change the contract to reflect the processes that you both believe work for the project. This is what you achieve through high levels of collaboration. The project leader should rigorously seek out processes that just don't work for the contract and make every effort to get those processes changed or removed. At the end of the day, the goal is to be effective and successful rather than follow processes for their own sake. The project is then managed with the contract.

The below steps must be adopted to produce a robust contract to ensure the collaboration is successful.

a. A contract is drafted during the tender phase.

b. On selection of the supplier, the supplier and the client review the contract to identify areas that may create conflicts and agree on how to address them. Not all issues may be resolved comfortably for everyone, and people shouldn't expect that to be the case. Procedures created for large infrastructure projects may not work for a particular package. These should be changed, if possible, for the smooth running of the project. The supplier may have other, better, already established procedures, and these could be adopted. However, some procedures required by the governance of large infrastructure projects cannot be changed for a specific package. The team, in such cases, should agree to operate with these.

c. A workshop should then be held in which the supplier and client go through the contract and ensure that their understanding of the contract is the same. Let the supplier review the contract and provide comments on their understanding. Contract language and interpretation can be clarified to prevent future conflicts in the contract.

d. Risk allocation should be clear, and there should be no disagreement at the outset of the contract. There should be no unaddressed conflicts on risk allocation. Clients sometimes try to push all the risk on the supplier. Note that this just comes back to you in the form of cost or results in fights down the line. If you choose a target-cost contract, then you pay anyway. Remember: the client bears the risk, regardless of where it sits. You just pay for it in a different form. Therefore, risks should be allocated fairly and to those who are best suited to address them.

e. The contract should then be signed and implemented. At no time should the contract be put in the drawer. However, the project manager will need to use discretion at times.

Implementing a contract doesn't mean you don't exercise discretion. Remember that small favours and a bit of flexibility on the side of the client will go a long way towards making your project a success. The fact that it is the supplier's responsibility doesn't mean the client shouldn't help if it is within their capability. The contract will clearly state who is responsible, so that should not be up for debate. If it is in the client's power to make the action a success, the client should take action for the overall success of the project. However, the supplier should not take advantage of the client's willingness to support.

I cannot emphasise enough the importance of developing a robust contract and implementing it. However, a robust contract does not mean that it will be able to predict everything in the future. A good robust contract is one that is flexible enough to accommodate changes, as there are likely to be a few on a project. Some projects will go to the extent of amending all standard clauses but provide inadequate information on the scope of the work and the governance required to undertake the work. Others will also be so specific in everything that the contract becomes an explosion waiting to happen. A robust contract should be clear, fair in terms of allocation of risk, and flexible enough to accommodate change. Developing a robust contract requires a deep understanding of the project and what is required to deliver it, the maturity of the scope, the interfaces, the type of project, extensive lessons learnt, and the various stakeholders involved. Many projects have gone into crisis because lawyers have been employed to draft contract documentation for work that they have no knowledge about. The right people need to be involved in developing contract documentation. One of the best books I have read for background on what not to do when developing contract documentation is by Nicholas J. Carnell, a solicitor. His book *Causation and Delay in Construction Disputes* is a must-read for every infrastructure project leader.

The project manager should set up the contract in such a way that ensures that the contractor will be successful. Every incentive you put in the contract should help the contractor to win that incentive. If the contractor is successful, the project will be successful.

Given the complexity of large infrastructure projects, there will be situations when following the governance process may be detrimental to the overall success of the project. In such cases, there will be a need to be flexible and bypass certain processes. This should be weighed carefully before making such a decision. The question to ask yourself during such a scenario is 'Will the risk of breaking the governance process be far smaller than the risk of not being flexible?' This decision should be taken with your sponsor or assigned senior manager. This scenario is not unusual for complex or large infrastructure projects.

Right Behaviours

The contract is critical for a collaborative relationship to be successful in the construction of infrastructure projects. However, if you just leave it at developing an agreeable contract, you are likely to descend into bickering over what the contract states. You will soon end up with low levels of collaboration and at the transactional end of the spectrum. This will then most likely lead to the project going into crisis, as there are bound to be changes on complex projects which will require quick decisions and reactions from both parties. As experienced project managers will tell you, the response time for NEC contracts may not even help you in such a case. There needs to be a relationship among the leaders who can drive some amount of flexibility in the contract and still implement the contract at the same time.

Realise the Different Cultures

The leaders should realise they have different cultures and ways of working. The different ways of working can cause strain on the relationship, with some teams reverting to their own type once the honeymoon period is over. Therefore, the joint leadership team, right from the start, should set the rules and values on how the project team will operate. The joint leadership team should commit themselves to driving the right behaviours throughout the project to ensure its success.

The leaders should spend the first three months agreeing on communication plans, escalation procedures, how conflicts will be addressed, how collaboration will be measured, and on delivering their commitments to gain trust. At the same time, the leaders should be flexible and understand that the relationship is in its embryonic stages and that room should be allowed for errors. However, wrong behaviours should be stamped out as soon as they rear their head.

Model the Right Behaviours

The leaders should model the behaviours they want the team to emulate. They should not engage in any discussions which smack of backbiting or seem to suggest underperformance of their partner with their team members. Even if the project leader suspects that is the case, they should deal with it directly with the supplier's leader. Once the leader starts behaviour contrary to what is expected, the team will follow suit, and the relationship will be on a downward spiral.

Show Empathy

Some team members will complain about the suppliers without viewing the issue from the supplier's perspective. They may be apprehensive about their own ability to deliver and try to find a scapegoat for their own failure. Some simply do not have the emotional intelligence to deal with the situation. Whatever the case may be, such issues should be stamped out. I have had a couple of project managers who complained about one thing after another only to realise that the issues were actually being addressed by the supplier. I once had to show our team Dan Ariely's 'What makes us feel good about our work?' One of the things he discovered from his experiment was that if you keep tearing people's work down, you invariably destroy their motivation for them to do any better. The same reaction occurs when you ignore the good work that people do. Criticising the supplier's work continuously will lead to a downhill spiral.

The motivational requirements of appreciating people's work, letting them find meaning in the work that they do, ownership, pride, challenge, and identity apply across the board. The supplier needs encouragement and support, not criticism. In the chapter on project leadership, I discuss methods of team motivation such as celebrating milestones and having team events together, which is applicable here.

Know Your Limits

On the extreme end, some client team members, in the spirit of collaboration, will take over the main supplier's work and start communicating with their subcontractors, confusing the contract since they do not understand what the main supplier has contracted to their suppliers. This is not ideal and should be discouraged as it will cause the project to descend into crisis.

Be Fair With Supplier, Allow Him to Settle and Consider Long-Term

Sometimes clients do not allow suppliers to settle in before they start making strenuous demands, some of which may even be outside the contract. They then start accusing the supplier of underperformance. A strong project leader should be ready to defend their supplier. You should be fair and give the supplier a chance, regardless of the backlash you may face. In the long run, this will lead to a stronger relationship and ensure a successful delivery. At times, I have been criticised for standing by my supplier; however, it has always paid off in the long run. It doesn't mean being soft — it is about being fair, firm, and considering the long-term vision and goals.

Manage Change and Surprises

Also, too many changes from the client can cause the supplier to feel demotivated. For example, a supplier is given a set of dates for getting access to the site, and they produce a programme. Then, as soon as they schedule the activities to reflect the changes, the dates are revised again by the client. When these changes continue, the supplier's team may get demotivated to push on with the work. The client team gets discouraged and complains that the supplier is not performing — not understanding how much they have contributed

157

to this. You need a strong leadership team to drive the right behaviours during this time.

Allow Time for the Team to Bond

The project leadership team should understand that the project team (clients and supplier) will all go through the process of Forming, Storming, Norming, and Performing. They should guide this process to ensure that it doesn't descend into bickering and fighting. The team needs time to go through all these stages, and the process should not be rushed. At the Forming stage, team members at each level should get to know their counterparts in the other organisations and start building a relationship of their own. This is where the team needs to start understanding what collaboration means to them and their different ways of working. Every relationship starts slowly as you make the conscious effort of allowing the other party to succeed whilst you build trust.

During the early stages of the contract, conflicts will arise; it happens in every Storming phase. Do not brush the reasons for these under the carpet, as they will rear their head at a later stage and disrupt the project. Rather, acknowledge them and address the conflicts head on and quickly. You sometimes hear the client team say after the preferred bidder has been chosen or contract signed, 'They have changed their behaviours'. Sometimes I sit the supplier's leader down to discuss this — and they say the same thing! Everyone's perspective is their truth. Rather than having these chats behind closed doors, sit the various teams down and discuss the issues; set them right quickly, and do not let them fester. The client and supplier teams should make an effort to solve problems together when issues come up rather than pointing fingers or resorting to a blame culture. This will strengthen the project team and drive the right behaviours across the board.

Develop a Win-Win Mentality

Also, remember that a 'Winners vs Losers' mentality causes projects to go into crisis. Each team tries to get one over the other to feel smart. This is driven by bad leadership. The attitude for driving behaviours on the project should be a win-win mentality, where parties push to ensure that both parties win in all cases.

The leaders of the various organisations are crucial in how the project teams will behave. Projects have gone sour because the leaders on both sides have a history, and they don't want to collaborate with each other. Although the immediate team tries to collaborate, the relationship finally breaks down. There may be other causes, but lack of collaboration invariably contributes to the relationship deteriorating to the level that it can result in a change in the supplier.

A Strong Collaborative Leadership

As explained in the preface of this book, strong collaborative leadership is what is required for success in delivering a complex project — either the whole project or a package of the large infrastructure project.

To be able to implement a robust contract, be flexible, and drive the right behaviours, one requires a strong collaborative leadership skillset to make the project successful. The leadership skills required to manage a collaborative relationship across the project, which includes the supplier's team, is significantly different from that required to manage the team in your organisation. Remember that they have a different culture and are driven by different objectives. Also, you don't have that direct positional power to push the supplier's team to do what you want. Relying solely on the contract will lead to a transactional relationship, with the project likely descending into crisis.

The leader should be specifically skilled in the following areas:

- » Solid influencing skills.

- » Powerful motivational skills.

- » Ability to build relationships across the board, from the leadership team of the supplier right through to their supply chains.

- » Ability to identify and handle conflicts that the different cultures of the organisations will create without creating a rift in the relationship.

- » Ability to manage upwards effectively in their own organisation and able to influence their own seniors to exhibit the right behaviours. This, at times, may require being firm with seniors.

- » Ability to accept when his/her organisation is wrong and be fair in all dealings. No one likes a client who tries to bulldoze their way through and cover up when it is clear they are in the wrong.

- » Effective communication skills.

- » Ability to be calm in stressful situations and to provide confidence in others.

- » Strong emotional intelligence skills.

- » Ability to share control with the supplier's leadership team.

There are some things that you should do as a project leader leading a collaborative work environment and others that you shouldn't. Most of these have been discussed throughout this book. These things are important for leadership as a whole on a complex project but critical if you are trying to improve the collaborative levels in the relationship. The following are the critical things to pay attention to:

- Learn how to gain buy-in for your vision. You need to be able to be good at selling the vision, ideas, and ways of working with the team. As mentioned previously, you do not directly pay the salaries of the staff of the supplier. The tools to motivate them and gain buy-in are different. I don't subscribe to the theory that leaders pay people salaries to be their motivators. Those leaders are not skilled enough to manage complex infrastructure projects. Instead, let people do it because they believe in it and want to achieve this for the team and themselves.

- No Blame Culture. As a former project director of mine used to say, 'No Victims!' As I discussed in the chapter on Reactive Troubleshooting, things do go wrong on complex infrastructure projects. When they go wrong, people already know who is at fault, and there is no need to drum it continuously into everyone's ears. Doing that will put people on the defensive and may even stop people from trying other innovative solutions for fear of getting it wrong and being in trouble. When challenges rear their head, get together and work out solutions on how to resolve the issue; the contract will deal with the cost later. This will improve the relationship and get people to trust you more and sometimes even feel they owe you a favour which will be returned in the future. Always think about the long-term consequence of your behaviours and not only your short-term wins. A Blame Culture will impact productivity, morale, and, ultimately, your project outcomes. When things are going well, encourage the contractor.

- Empathy is key to your success. You always need to try to understand what it feels like to be the supplier or the client. That will enable you to make better decisions. Building relationships across the board is key to your success. Being able to see it from the other person's point of view will help you make better decisions that will improve trust on the project.

- Patience is a virtue. I mentioned previously how some clients do not give the supplier the chance to settle and deliver. You need to learn patience. Give people time; not every little thing should make you scream and shout. There are certain things — just as there are in a marriage — that you need to let go and not talk about. If you complain and talk about everything, people stop taking you seriously.

- Monitor the progress of the culture in the team. This should be undertaken using surveys. The surveys should ask the following questions:

  » Are we modelling the right behaviours?

  » Are we being fair to each other?

  » Are we acting in accordance with the collaboration levels we have agreed on with our supplier?

  » Are our joint vision and goals clear?

  » Are we exhibiting our values?

  » Are the supplier and client leadership operating as a joint team?

  » Do we trust each other?

- Give credit where it is due. Give credit to the other party even if you believe the success was due to you. These days, people even use social media to give credit to their suppliers. You should use the same methods for working jointly in solving problems to share the success and blow the supplier's horn accordingly. This will boost morale and increase trust in the client-supplier relationship.

- Model the desired behaviours throughout the project. Use those times when things go wrong to stand firm and truly model the behaviours and values you have adopted. The team will follow this when they witness it.

- Be fair but firm. There are some leaders who are very aggressive and just live to quarrel. And there are some who, in the guise of collaboration, will try to avoid all forms of conflict. They will then join their team and badmouth the contractor. And there is that one person who just sits on the fence all the time. You really don't want any of these project leaders to be running a complex infrastructure project, let alone a collaborative relationship.

Always remember that the reason that the project was commissioned was to deliver the required goals. Never lose sight of that. If people continue to fail to deliver their part of their bargain, then, of course, there is no need for collaboration. You are collaborating for a purpose, and that purpose needs to be achieved. So, although you need to be patient, fair, have empathy, and all of that, you need to be able to tackle non-performance head on and challenge your partner effectively to ensure they are delivering their part of their bargain. If you are not able to do this, sooner or later people will get fed up with the relationship, and the project will descend into crisis. If you have developed very solid personal relationships with your partner, you can tackle conflicts head on and take drastic measures, and your partner will understand you and have no issues. However, when you are being direct and tackling a problem, remember that you need to focus on the issue and what is not being done or done wrong. Do not attack the character of the individuals. You need to deal with the conflict in a calm, unemotional way.

Making the Collaboration Successful

Making the collaboration successful is making your project success-ful. Although the plan is to have a robust contract in place, no con-tract is 'water-tight', and so you need to be flexible and able to devel-op a project team that can react quickly to change. As the contract progresses and the initial excitement dies down, people will want to resort to the ways of working that they know. New people will join the team who will want to make their mark on the project, bringing some disruption to the team. Major changes in the project may oc-cur that will require robustness — and, at the same time, flexibility — of each partner. The team should be ready to move beyond this and still be effective in delivering, with high levels of collaboration.

We did state that true collaboration is difficult, and this is due to the following:

- Dealing with people. Dealing with people is difficult. Each one has their own experiences and behaviour. They also have their own vision of what they believe they should be doing and heading towards.

- Different organisational cultures. People not only have unique behaviours and idiosyncrasies, but they also have a set way of working in their various organisations, which make them different from you.

- Money. This is the number-one factor that causes relation-ship nightmares, and projects are no different. In a large infrastructure project, you are dealing with huge sums, some of which are bigger than some countries' GDPs.

These sums can cause the collapse of suppliers if they get it wrong, leading to the loss of livelihood of their workers.

- Change in projects. Most people don't react well to change, but large infrastructure projects sometimes bring huge changes that can be disruptive to the companies involved and even to people's personal lives.

It is important to realise that these are what will influence 99% of the behaviours that you will have to deal with on the project. By being aware of this, you will tend not to take things too personally and understand how those people feel.

Building a solid relationship to improve trust is what will ensure that the right behaviours are demonstrated on the project. And so, the goal of the project team in a highly collaborative working environment is to build relationships across the board and to increase the trust index.

The following diagram, from Stephen M. R. Covey's The Speed of Trust, indicates how important trust is to a project:

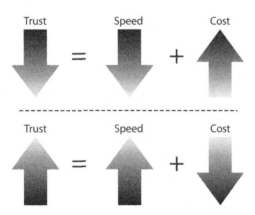

The following are some of the things you need to do to build solid relationships and increase the trust index:

- Create a charter on the ways of working for the project. The charter should state clearly why the project is being undertaken and how members are expected to act and behave. Create a charter together that everyone can be committed to, and let people sign the document. If possible, include the charter in the contract if everyone agrees.

- Create quick wins that will allow the team to work on an issue together to help develop the relationship.

- Ensure there is a transition period, in which the team is allowed to settle into the new ways of working. The period for this should be clearly communicated to the team to allow everyone to settle in and then start to deliver.

- There should be a project board, with clear roles and responsibilities for the project.

- Undertake joint-leadership programmes and have a coach on board who everyone can speak to. This will improve their collaborative skills and also their emotional intelligence.

- Celebrate milestones together.

- Use 360 reviews to assess the health of the relationship and address concerns.

- Endeavour to sit together in the same building with the teams from the various organisations. It is difficult for people to backbite people they sit with.

- Encourage team members to develop personal relationships with their opposite counterparts. A friend is more likely to support you in times of crisis.

- Do what you said you would do. To improve trust, you need to do what you said you would do, no matter how unimportant you feel that issue is.

- Use times when things go wrong to improve trust between the client and the supplier by working together to address the problems, regardless of whose fault it is.

- Key meetings should always be attended by the leaders. After a while, project leaders start sending delegates to certain critical meetings. This shows disrespect and sows mistrust. There are certain key meetings that the project leaders should never delegate, if possible, and always attend to keep the relationship going.

Relationship building should be the work of everyone, not just the leader. Leaders should, however, set the example by encouraging their counterparts to build relationships across the board.

Project leaders should spend most of their time building relationships across the board and speaking to the team to know their fears. Try to build a relationship across the supplier chain if the main supplier is comfortable. I have realised in the past that I found out about issues which we could address before they became big problems. However, this should be done with care and agreement with the main supplier, as it can cause mistrust if the main supplier feels that you are undermining them.

The typical day for a leader should be going around and speaking to individuals throughout the hierarchy to understand the next issue that they need to resolve and find out what they can do to help. Sometimes being open to hearing their fears and worries is good enough. The leaders should work hard to create an environment where all sides feel confident to share mistakes they have made and worries they have without fear of repercussions or being penalised. Archer and Cameron's Collaborative Leadership suggests facilitating regular, confidential risk workshops where senior leaders from all sides can talk openly about their worst fears and the risks they see in their various organisations. The leaders should realise that no problem is too small to track. The small, niggling worry that you fail to track may become your biggest nightmare.

In making the relationship successful, it is OK to start from a transactional end of the spectrum for the team to start delivering to gain trust and increase the levels of collaboration as the relationship matures. As the project and relationship move on successfully towards the completion of the project, it sometimes becomes difficult to keep the energy levels up to close the project. Every experienced project leader is aware that most accidents on the construction site occur, getting to the end of the project. Also, the high levels of energy required to close an infrastructure project, document the lessons learnt, and complete the Health and Safety file close to the end of the project may be lacking. During this time, it is OK to be a bit more transactional in your dealings to complete the project safely and on time.

If the Relationship Doesn't Work, Leave Amicably

At times, a relationship may fail, and you will need to replace the supplier. This is unfortunate, and I have had to deal with such a scenario before. This may be due to reasons beyond the control of either partner. At this time, a transition plan is also required to transition the new supplier into place. It is important not to badmouth the incumbent supplier to the new supplier. Some project leaders take pride in doing this to justify their actions. All you are doing is sowing mistrust in your new supplier. They will begin the project feeling they may meet the same end and will, therefore, not want to collaborate and be very wary of the client. The relationship with the incumbent supplier should also not be cut off abruptly. Leaders should try to keep the relationship going and not burn bridges. By keeping up the collaborative relationship with the incumbent supplier, you increase the chances of the incumbent supplier collaborating with the incoming supplier to ensure there is a successful transition.

Conclusion of Chapter

Collaboration is a bit misunderstood in the industry, easy to talk about yet difficult to implement. All infrastructure projects are in some form of collaborative working, although the levels of collaboration may be low. High levels of collaboration are required to enable large and complex infrastructure projects to be successful.

The three pillars of a robust contract, right behaviours, and a strong collaborative leadership together with the tools discussed under 'making the collaboration successful' are critical to the success of a project.

Chapter 10:

Lean Philosophy

To deliver complex projects or large infrastructure projects successfully, you want to deliver as efficiently as you can to increase your chances of attaining the criteria that will make you successful. If you think about it, no project progresses with the intention of including waste. All projects want to deliver as efficiently as possible. However, if you do not make a conscious effort or have a mindset of driving waste out of the project, you may have good intentions, but you are not necessarily delivering efficiently. Many projects make an effort in this direction, even without calling it 'lean philosophy or management'. On a project I was involved in, several of us were nominated to achieve yellow belt in Lean Six Sigma. This involved reviewing existing procedures and improving them by removing waste and making them more efficient.

Lean-philosophy mindset, not just the tools, is one every complex or large infrastructure projects should adopt to help effectively drive out waste.

Lean-management philosophy is derived from the Japanese manufacturing industry. The philosophy is made synonymous to the Toyota Production System (TPS) although the two have some differences.

TPS, which was developed by Taiichi Ohno and his team, came about when they studied the Ford production system, and it occurred to them that a series of simple innovations might make it possible to provide both continuity in process flow and a greater variety in products. Ford's system did not allow variety of products.

The term 'Lean' was coined by James P Womack, Daniel T Jones, and Daniel Roos in their influential book titled 'The Machine That Changed the World: The Story of Lean Production'.

Lean Thinking (1996) by James P Womack, Daniel Roos, and Daniel T. Jones, distilled the following as the five principles of Lean:

1. Specify the value desired by the customer.
2. Identify the value stream for each product providing that value, and challenge all of the wasted steps (generally nine out of ten) currently necessary to provide it.
3. Make the product flow continuously through the remaining value-added steps.
4. Introduce pull between all steps where continuous flow is possible.
5. Manage toward perfection so that the number of steps and the amount of time and information needed to serve the customer continually falls.

In an article published by Bob Emiliani on April 3, 2016, he highlights a few differences and places high importance on the human aspect. He stated that TPS places a lot more emphasis on the following than Lean:

1. Continuous Improvement
2. Respect for people
3. Management-employee relations

4. Mutual trust and teamwork

5. Stable employment

6. Human energy, enthusiasm, and passion for improvement

7. Evolution in mindset and methods

8. Infinite possibilities for improvement

9. Hunger for survival

A bit of research will tell you that Toyota has been the largest car automaker in terms of sales for years now. Their focus on the human, relationship-building, and team-working principles may be key to their pulling ahead of everyone. These are the principles that large or complex infrastructure projects will need to adopt whilst they focus on the Lean principles.

According to Jeffery Liker (author of the book The Toyota Way), the Toyota Way is supported by two main pillars — continuous improvement, sometimes referred to as Kaizen, and respect for people. Continuous improvement requires the creation of an environment that embraces change and causes employees to be comfortable enough to challenge everything. Jeffery Liker says, 'Such an environment can be created only where there is respect for people, hence, the second pillar of the Toyota Way. Toyota demonstrates this respect by providing employment security and seeking to engage team members through active participation in improving their jobs'.

For a complex or large infrastructure project to be successful (on budget, on time, employees more fulfilled and learning new skills), these two pillars should be implemented rigorously. The project should be looking to continuously improve their ways of working.

Continuous Improvement means that leaders allow their teams to challenge a system that doesn't work, which frustrates and demotivates them. Challenging the system then will enable them to bring those gems of ideas that will ensure the success of the project.

On many projects, if you speak to the team about Lean, they will inform you that they are already using Lean and that there is nothing different you can add. However, we realise that these projects are not more successful than others. They assume that, since they are using the tools of Lean, they should be reaping similar benefits. If you dig deeper, you will realise that the pillars of Continuous Improvement and an environment in which the team is respected and developed enough to enable them to continuously challenge the system does not exist in either the project financers, project owners, clients, or the senior team. So, what they are applying is a superficial Lean, which does not accept change to ensure they reap all the benefits of Lean. So, the tools taught by several Lean gurus are really not the reason for the success of Toyota. Rather, it is their management's commitment to continuously invest in its people and promote a culture of continuous improvement. Remember, in a previous chapter, we discussed that if we focused on the human factor a bit more, the triangle of cost, time, and quality will be OK.

Adopt the Right Principles for Your Project Based on Best Practices

The Toyota Way 14 principles, although created for a manufacturing context, are applicable to all large infrastructure projects and can be a great asset to project leaders, project owners, and clients in large infrastructure projects. For Lean to be successful, its philosophy needs to be adopted throughout the organisation — not just in the construction team or onsite.

The diagram below demonstrates how each principle builds on the previous one. To ensure success on the principles, one has to follow through with the whole process.

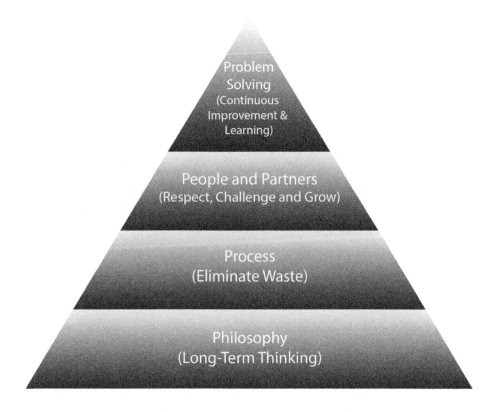

Fig 10.1 The 4P Model of the Toyota Way

The 14 principles, grouped under the 4P model, are:

Philosophy: Long-Term Thinking

Principle 1: Base management decisions on a long-term philosophy, even at the expense of short-term financial goals.

This should start at the concept stage of the project and continue through the lifecycle of the project. As you recall, we discussed in the chapter on risk the importance of understanding the risk profile and the risk introduced with every decision that you make on the project.

Process: Eliminate Waste

Principle 2: Create continuous process flow to bring problems to the surface.

Principle 3: Use 'pull' systems to avoid over-production

This works well on a construction site to avoid clutter, damage to materials, increase space to work, and, therefore, achieve more efficiency. Certain items may need to be given a bit more time to be delivered ahead of time due to the risk consequence of not arriving in time. You need to review this and make the judgement.

Principle 4: Level out the workload (work like the tortoise, not the hare).

Principle 5: Build a culture of stopping to fix problems, getting the right quality correct the first time.

Principle 6: Standardise tasks as a foundation for continuous improvement and empowerment.

All work should be standardised as much as possible — in the office as well as on the construction site.

Principle 7: Use visual control so problems are not hidden.

Project plans, schedules, critical paths, and EV metrics should be made visual on walls and boards. Teams should use these methods to discuss the schedules, discuss the work for flushing out problems, and find solutions.

Principle 8: Use reliable, tested technology that serves your people and processes.

It's heartbreaking when projects use technology that plainly doesn't work. Document-control systems are sometimes the culprit. Seek out tried-and-tested technology that works to ensure your team is working as efficiently as possible.

People and Partners: Respect, Grow, Challenge

Principle 9: Grow leaders who understand the work, live the philosophy, and teach others.

On large infrastructure projects, you don't need one leader — you need several of them. To make your project successful, you need to delegate to the lowest possible level so that decisions can be quick. No leader should be a bottleneck for decisions. The leader's responsibility on the project is to grow several more leaders with the same philosophy. The Hinkley Point C Nuclear project had a leadership lanyard programme that helped to develop leaders with similar values that they wanted for the project.

Principle 10: Develop exceptional people and teams who follow your philosophy.

Principle 11: Respect your extended network of partners by challenging them and helping them to improve.

Respect your suppliers and the several stakeholders on the project; they are the ones who will make you successful. If you respect them, they will respond to you in kind, and the project is likely to be more successful.

Problem Solving: Continuous Improvement & Learning

Principle 12: Go and see to thoroughly understand the situation.

Try to understand the situations with your suppliers and stakeholders, don't form opinions without knowing the facts. What is causing the milestones to be missed or targets not being met both in the office on the construction site? Seek to understand the situation thoroughly.

Principle 13: Make decisions slowly by consensus, considering all options, and implement rapidly.

This is not an excuse for not making decisions because if you don't make a choice, then you have already made a decision. However, think through the consequences of your decisions and test them with colleagues before implementing them. An extreme example is replacing a supplier on a project. Such decisions need to be thought through carefully and thoroughly.

Principle 14: Become a learning organisation through relentless reflection and continuous improvement.

Everything you do should be about continuous learning throughout the project right up until completion. The team should be equipped with the confidence of challenging processes and finding better ways of doing the work. Do not be reckless, though.

The above Toyota Principles are a great starting point; however, every complex project will need to develop its own set of principles that will make them successful. A culture of continuous learning and an environment where people are respected enough so they can challenge the system are, however, critical.

An example of the right principles for a company based on trust and an environment that allows for mistakes and continuous improvement is Bridgewater Associates, founded by Ray Dalio. Bridgewater Associates is the largest hedge fund in the world and the fifth-most-important private company in the US (according to *For-*

tune). Dalio, who created this company from his two-bedroom apartment in 1975, is currently one of the most successful people on this earth. In his book *Principles — Life and Work*, he lists the following principles:

- Principle 1: Trust in radical truth and radical transparency

- Principle 2: Cultivate meaningful work and meaningful relationships

- Principle 3: Create a culture in which it is OK to make mistakes and unacceptable not to learn from them

- Principle 9: Constantly train, test, evaluate, and sort people

- Principle 12: Diagnose problems to get at their root causes

- Principle 15: Use tools and protocols to shape how work is done

The basic principle of tailoring to suit the specific needs of each project is key. However, Lean Philosophy is something that can be adopted for every project, specifically the pillars of continuous improvement and respect for people. This is seen in Bridgewater's principles as well, which has made them very successful. The need to improve the trust index and remove any backbiting is also portrayed in the Bridgewater principles, as we have already discussed.

Using Only the Lean Tools Does Not Guarantee Success

Taiichi Ohno, who is credited with creating TPS, studied Ford's book *Today and Tomorrow*. The Ford book taught standardising processes and eliminating waste.

Taiichi Ohno also studied the pull system from American supermarkets who stocked their shelves only when the products were gone. He also took to heart the teachings of the American quality pioneer W. Edwards Deming. This means they learnt most of the principles from the Americans and yet had to go and teach these principles to bail out the Ford Company in America. This tells us that applying the tools alone is not enough to guarantee success.

The view of the Toyota management is that they build people, not just cars. This poses the question to project leaders: 'Are you just about hitting milestones and completing the project without really caring about developing the people and taking care of their mental health, or are you happy in developing your team to the point that you trust them to make the right decisions, challenge your systems, and create improvement in the systems?'

When Jeffery Liker interviewed the senior manager of Toyota for his book *The Toyota Way*, he asked them why Toyota existed as a business. He mentions that their responses were remarkably consistent. For example, Jim Press, Executive Vice President and C.O.O. of Toyota Motor Sales in North America and one of two American Managing Directors of Toyota, explained:

'The purpose of the money we make is not for us as a company to gain, and it's not for us as associates to see our stock portfolio grow or anything like that. The purpose is so we can reinvest in the future, so we can continue to do this. That's the purpose of our investment. And to help society and to help the community, and to contribute back to the community that we're fortunate enough to do business in. I've got a trillion examples of that.'

This speaks to the vision that you create for the project. It means that the ultimate vision of the project should contribute to society. Every project does this; however, project owners are sometimes not good at selling this vision. The vision we develop that will drive the project to success should go beyond just meeting the immediate goals of cost, quality, and time.

Furthermore, Liker mentions that Toyota discusses seven major types of non-value-added waste in business or manufacturers' processes. However, he added an eighth, which is intriguing to me. He calls it 'unused employee creativity' — losing time, ideas, skills, improvements, and learning opportunities by not engaging or listening to your employees.

The goal is to have a philosophy that empowers your team so they can challenge the system and seek improvements continuously. The focus needs to be more on the people and trusting them to do the work.

Making Lean Management Work for You

Liker says that most business processes are 90% waste and 10% value-added work. We are all aware of the processes, procedures, and duplication of efforts in large infrastructure projects that add no value to the projects.

Also, suppliers are sometimes asked to meet targets which make for double handling and unnecessary storage, resulting in damage to the products. Sometimes these are pushed through because certain non-critical targets need to be met due to media pressure. Costs escalate through waste, and important targets of the project are missed.

The Lean philosophy is about using the right process and procedures to deliver things right the first time. Activities that are wasteful should be done away with and the ways of working continuously reviewed and improved. Therefore, for Lean to be successful in the construction industry, I believe that three critical things need to be present in the large infrastructure environment:

1. Client leadership adopting the Lean philosophy and culture over meeting non-critical targets or adopting the cheapest price during tender. This ensures trust in the supply chain, which is vital to the success of the Lean principles. The client needs to adopt the Lean strategy for tender, which will dictate how they intend to procure the supply chain.

2. Supplier collaboration, which we discussed in the previous chapter. This will ensure that the Lean philosophy is adopted throughout the supply chain to ensure reducing waste and smoothing of processes.

3. Information Technology tools like BIM that will facilitate the smooth transfer of information and help reduce waste.

For Lean to be successful, the leadership should be open to questioning. Through rigorous examination of the processes, procedures, and the reasons for certain targets or products, waste can be reduced and the system perfected. These three points are yet another confirmation that smart project leadership is important in achieving success on an infrastructure project.

The Lean philosophy is not limited just to the main supplier and the client. The Lean philosophy enables the whole system (including all suppliers involved in the project) to adopt a lean mindset so that the system behaves and runs as one, reducing waste and seeking to continuously improve.

Areas for Waste-Reduction Opportunities in Large Infrastructure Projects

Large infrastructure projects sometimes carry significant waste, due to duplication of effort. Sometimes people are not clear on what others may be doing. Different packages may not learn from other packages and keep recreating the same things. In the effort to standardise, certain processes are adopted for packages on large infrastructure projects, which are not necessarily suited for that particular package.

Below are five areas that you can focus your attention on to reduce waste.

1. Client processes and procedures. Most large infrastructure projects have several processes and procedures that normally don't work or are not applicable to specific suppliers or particular packages that form part of the large infrastructure project. However, due to standardisation of the large infrastructure project, project leaders will sometimes push their suppliers to get on with it anyway. This causes frustration for the suppliers and a lot of waste of resources and time.

2. Review deliverables for whether they add value. There are several deliverables (reports, documents, milestones, etc.) which sometimes add no value to the final products. However, project managers are sometimes worried about challenging their superiors and will push their suppliers to deliver these just to satisfy seniors. Sometimes the same deliverables will be asked for in several different formats.

3. Reviewing construction processes to reduce waste. The construction industry is good at this; however, not all projects implement this enough. Once they start with a process, they will normally stick to it without actually finding ways to improve the process continuously.

4. Ensuring that all parties (designers, tier 1 contractors, and the whole supplier chain) deliver on their promises to ensure that there is workflow from one party to another without any standing time. This will require an integrated

schedule that all parties (client, designers, tier 1 contractors, and entire supply chain) work to meet.

5. Reduce over-design. Rigorously investigate the design to ensure that it has not been over-designed, as the knock-on effect of materials and plant required to install the design is huge.

6. Invest in your team's development so they can identify other waste streams to reduce, which will help ensure the success of the project.

Lean Construction

According to Construction Excellence, Lean construction is a philosophy based on the concepts of lean manufacturing. It is about managing and improving the construction process to profitably deliver what the customer needs.

The Lean Construction Institute Triangle tries to capture this requirement. The triangle has as its sides Organisation (integrated organisation), Commercial (align commercial interests), and Operating System (lean management tools).

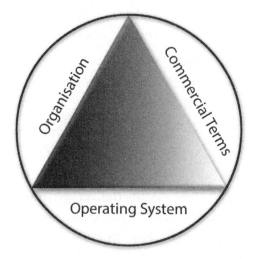

Fig 10.2 The Lean Construction Institute triangle

Organisation

This calls for integrated organisations with an integrated governance. This implies integrating not just the designer and tier 1 contractor but all the way down to the fabricators and installers.

I believe the concept is a great one that we should aspire to achieve. However, on a mega infrastructure project, where you may have several players and different specialities on board, this may be difficult to achieve. For example, if you consider the requirements for a nuclear power station or a project like HS2 in the United Kingdom, this may not be easily achievable. If you consider how funding is obtained for mega projects, this may not be an easy call; however, we still need to aspire to this. This will require a mindset change starting with the government and organisations funding complex projects. However, an integrated structure for the individual packages involving the client, designers, tier 1 contractor, and critical tier 2 contractors is a start that we can readily achieve.

The alliance model is geared towards this; however, I will not recommend any particular model over another, as I believe every method should be tailored to the project according to its complexity and risks.

Commercial Terms

To ensure that this integration works efficiently and that behaviours are consistent with the client's interests and priorities, the Lean Construction Institute proposes a set of agreements known as Integrated Project Delivery (IPD) or Integrated Form of Agreements (IFOA). IPD intends to create an alignment of the interests of all parties in the project with the clients' goals and objectives. This calls for selecting partners based on culture and technical fit rather than 'The cheapest supplier gets the job' mentality.

Operating System

There are several Lean Management tools or techniques which can be used in the large infrastructure environment. The tools are sometimes used in isolation; however, more benefit will be gained if these are combined. Some of these are:

1. 5S

    » Sort (eliminate that which is not needed)

    » Set in Order (Organise remaining items)

    » Shine (Clean and inspect work area)

    » Standardise (write standards for above)

    » Sustain (regularly apply the standards)

    One can see how this is easily applicable to the construction area for improving efficiency and eliminating hazards, making the work safer and more efficient.

2. Bottleneck Analysis. Identify which part of the process limits efficiency or dictates the programme, and find ways to improve this bottleneck. Note that this could be decision making bottleneck.

3. *Gemba* (The Real Place)

    A philosophy that reminds us to get out of the office and spend time on the construction site to understand the work being undertaken so we can make the right decisions. How many project leaders do you find sitting in their offices, never making it a point to visit the work areas to understand the constraints themselves and how to address these?

4. *Hoshin Kanri* (Policy Deployment)

    Align the goals of the company/project (strategy) with

the plans of middle management (tactics) and the work performed on the construction site.

5. Just-in-Time (JIT)

Pull parts through, based on demand, instead of pushing parts through to the site, based on projected demand. JIT should not be used, however, for items that carry a risk of an incident occurring during transportation and not being available when they are required. However, this process prevents costs associated with storage on site, prevents defects and cost due to double handling, and ensures a tidy workplace so that the work can progress speedily without incidents. This tool will work with the Kanban technique, in which things are called for only when needed.

6. *Kaizen* (Continuous Improvement)

A strategy where employees work together proactively to achieve regular, incremental improvements in the process. I will call this 'total collaboration among the project team (client and supplier chain) to achieve continuous improvements in the processes and throughout the work'.

I was on a project where we had to remove 22,000 cubic metres from a constrained area and install fill to be able to support a new railway track within a blockade in 6 days. The work involved removing the existing tracks and then working adjacent to live tracks. The constraints of the location made the work initially daunting; one supplier even stated that it was not possible. How we achieved this was to continuously review our process of removing the fill and installing the new fill and adjusting the process until we'd removed enough waste from our process to enable us to achieve our goal.

The construction of the Reading Elevated Railway Viaduct involved the pouring of 1.2km concrete deck spans. To help us achieve our targets, we wrote down the exact process from installing scaffolding, fixing steel, installing formwork, installing the bridge joints, pouring concrete, and striking formwork. We then followed this process through and identified where the process needed changing or tweaking, or was causing defects, etc., and improved it continuously. We ended up improving the process by 30%. This is not unique, as most projects focus on this, and there are several case studies on how this has saved several million on projects.

7. PDCA (Plan, Do, Check, Act)

This is an iterative methodology for implementing improvements:

- Plan (establish plan and expected results)

- Do (implement plan)

- Check (verify expected results achieved)

- Act (review and assess; do it again)

Fig 10.3 – The PDCA Cycle

8. Root-Cause Analysis

   This is a problem-solving methodology that focuses on identifying the actual problem in a case and not resorting to quick fixes of the symptoms. '5 Whys' and fishbone analysis are all root-cause analysis. We touched on this in the troubleshooting section. However, you need not wait for projects to be in crisis to use this. This is an ongoing process of troubleshooting issues that come up before they lead the project into crisis.

9. Standardised work

   Document best-practice procedures to be applied to the work front.

10. Value Stream Mapping

   A tool used to map the flow of production visually. This shows the current and future state of a process in a way that will highlight areas of the process that can be improved. Value stream mapping, often helps teams discover that steps can be eliminated, reorganised, or deferred in ways that will enhance the procedure, which then saves times and cost.

11. Target Value Design.

   This method is described in a CMAA document titled 'Managing Integrated Project Delivery'. This is a fantastic way to drive down over-design, drive value into the design, and prevent design that can't be constructed in large infrastructure projects. They list the major aspects of the process as below:

   • Rather than an estimate based on a detailed design, one should design based on a detailed estimate. That is the contractor, tradesmen, and the designer, through a joint effort, develop the design based on the client's requirement. Detailed estimates of this are then produced. The designer then designs to meet those detailed estimates.

- Rather than evaluate the constructability of the developed design, discuss with the builder (this could be the tier 2 or 3 contractor) what is buildable within the estimates before undertaking the detail design. At this stage, you will define the issues and provide the basis for the design.

The above are a few of the tools that are directly applicable; however, there are several tools in the industry that a project adopting the Lean philosophy can administer.

It is evident that, to deliver large infrastructure projects on time and within budget, one requires the adoption of a Lean Philosophy mindset. However, to be able to apply the Lean Philosophy to a project, one requires true collaboration with the entire project team, which requires adjustments to the procurement process/contract. For a true collaboration relationship to function properly, a collaborative and servant leader is needed. One should not focus solely on one and ignore the other.

In conclusion, one should remember the principles we have discussed about the success of Toyota and Bridgewater. The critical part of success is adopting your own principles — those that work for the project. However, this culture should be built on an environment of continuous improvement, trust across the board, investing in the development of your team, empowering your team, and promoting an environment in which the team can challenge the system and procedures with the goal of making it better. Such an environment, with a coaching and mentoring type of leadership, will empower people to make decisions and move the project towards success.

Chapter 11:

Project Leadership

'An army of sheep led by a lion will defeat an army of lions led by a sheep.'
— *Dr Myles Munroe*

Large infrastructure projects tend to be complex. Although the characteristics which make them complex require more of what is typically termed 'soft skills', they are actually the hard part, as most project management literature avoids delving deeply into them. If leadership skills are just common sense, why are they so hard to master?

The skills required to handle high public scrutiny, high media exposure, a large number of influential stakeholders, long durations — which means greater effort in keeping teams motivated — and multiple parties in the design and construction of the project go beyond standard project-management procedures. A large infrastructure project is not likely to lack technical expertise. Governance is key to a project's success, but so is knowing when the governance structures needs to be flexible.

Large infrastructure projects are often split into several packages, some of which are more than £1bn in value. Project managers of individual packages are not only dealing with several contractors but also interfacing with other package project managers who are also handling significant packages. Keeping in mind that you are not competing with the project manager handling the other package is sometimes a struggle in itself. Both of you want enough of the 'pie' for your project and are dealing with scope and impacts of interfacing work. All of them are trying to get noticed so they can get the support they need to be successful on the project.

The key to the successful delivery of large infrastructure projects is, therefore, great leadership throughout the lifecycle and across the board. The project doesn't need just one leader but several leaders with the right culture to make it successful. There should be a strong focus on recruiting leaders with the right mentality and behaviour. There should also be continuous development of leaders across the project, not limited only to project-management staff but engineers, the commercial team, planners, environmental team, etc.

The reason for this is that *leadership is everything* — and even more so in large infrastructure projects! Dr Myles Munroe stated that 'Nothing…

- happens without leadership

- changes without leadership

- develops without leadership

- improves without leadership

- is corrected without leadership

- advances without leadership

- succeeds without leadership

The UK Government has identified the need for strong leadership for complex projects. One of the Major Projects Authority's ('the Authority', now the Infrastructure and Projects Authority) top roles was to improve the capabilities of project leaders. It introduced the Major Projects Leadership Academy to develop the skills of senior leaders delivering complex projects.

As a leader of a complex project, your attitude and mentality will determine whether you will be successful or not. Your success on the project is dependent on 80% attitude/mentality and 20% on your technical skill. On a complex infrastructure project, you will have all the technical skills you require on the project. Therefore the 20% technical skill that you need may not be a problem. Your focus should be on getting the right sort of leadership skills. In the chapter on 'Supplier Collaboration', I discussed some of the attributes needed to ensure that the collaboration is successful.

I have been on several projects in which we told the stakeholders, including the contractor, what we wanted to achieve. In each case, we kept on selling our vision to everyone on the project until they all bought into it and did the impossible. Once people are bought into your vision and believe they can do it, they will find a way to reach the goal. You cannot achieve beyond your belief system. Your belief system determines your attitude, and your attitude determines the atmosphere on the project.

Using an analogy by Dr Myles Munroe, the lion is not the most intelligent, strongest, or biggest animal in the jungle; however, he causes the other animals to run scared. A lion looks at an elephant and sees lunch. The elephant sees the lion and sees itself as lunch, even though he is bigger and stronger. Your attitude is, therefore, everything, and, as a leader, your project's success depends on it.

The following are true of attitude:

- Your personal philosophy is your fundamental beliefs, concepts, and ideas

- What you say or feed yourself continuously will be embedded in your subconscious and forms your beliefs

- Attitude is the manifestation of your personal philosophy

- Attitude is a product of your belief

- No one can live beyond the limits of their beliefs

- Therefore, attitude determines your limitations

'People may hear your words, but they feel your ATTITUDE.' — *John C. Maxwell*

For centuries, it was believed that it was physically impossible to run a 4-minute mile. However, Roger Bannister made a mental shift and practised it several times in his mind until he absolutely believed that he could do it. He later would go out and shatter that myth. He knew he had to achieve this mentally before his body could do it. After Roger Bannister destroyed this myth, 37 people also ran a 4-minute mile within just two years. It is obvious that your mentality and belief system will determine your success in everything.

The project leader, therefore:

- Determines the mentality of the project team

- Determines the attitude of the project team

- Determines the commitment of the project team

- Determines the success of the project

'Leaders are people who do the right thing; managers are people who do things right.' — Professor Warren G. Bennis

This quote by Professor Warren G Bennis is insightful. Most people leading projects are managers and will do things right, but they won't necessarily do the right thing. Often managers pander to their bosses. They're thinking about their progression in the organisation and do not have enough vision to do the right thing for the project. Many projects go into crisis because they are led by managers and not by leaders.

As mentioned previously, the only things that are certain on large infrastructure projects are change, surprises, and tons of pressure. Therefore, what you need to deliver is excellent leadership skills — not excellent project-management skills. You should be someone who can help people believe the unbelievable, motivate people regardless of the situation, motivate yourself no matter how lonely you feel, and have loads of passion for what you do. Your goal is to create an environment that makes leaders on the project want to help push your vision forward and create engagement in the project team. Leadership is not about position, authority, social status, charisma or skill — it is about attitude and mentality. Your passion, your attitude, and commitment are what will attract your team to follow you.

Role of the Project Leadership

'Leadership is the capacity to influence others through inspiration generated by a passion motivated by a vision birthed by a conviction produced by a purpose.' — Dr Myles Munroe

True leaders are driven by conviction. They don't like power but are interested in empowering other people. Leadership is not about how many people serve you but the number of people you serve. This is extremely critical for large projects. A lot of people play politics in their drive to climb the corporate ladder. They don't understand why their projects fail, and they look for someone to blame. Great project leaders are those who are not interested in advancing themselves but advancing their team to achieve the vision of the project.

Project leaders should understand that everyone is a leader in their area of gifting. There is a difference between being a leader and developing your leadership skills. Several great leaders like Jesus Christ, Nelson Mandela, Martin Luther King, Abraham Lincoln, and Gandhi discovered themselves, identified their gifts, and followed a cause they were passionate about. They were prepared to go it alone and were not seeking people to follow them; people followed them because of their gift and their passion for their cause. Some of these people did not have what is identified in leadership books as leadership skills. A leader is recognised by their gift and passion. Leadership skills are developed from these.

If you fail to identify your gift and passion and focus on just developing leadership skills, you will revert to what you know best when the storm comes. This is the reason you see even acclaimed project leaders returning to nasty bickering, micromanaging, and a blame culture when difficulties arise. When your gift is identified and you are passionate about what you are doing, you become like an eagle. The storms only take you higher and helps to refine your leadership skills further.

The projects leader's role in a complex or large infrastructure project is, therefore, as follows:

- To build a team. It is vital to build the right team for that particular project, as described in Chapter 3.

- To create the vision. The Business Case will contain statistics and a cost-to-benefit ratio but not necessarily a vision for the project. The leader needs to create a vision for the project that takes into account the needs of the Business

Case. For large infrastructure projects made up of several packages, it is essential for the vision to be sold across all the packages. Some of the packages will have their own charters with refined mission statements specific to that package. But the overall project's vision should be central to any package's charter, and the package project manager should ensure this. Too many times, a package's scope and budget cause package leaders to focus on and care only about delivering their packages successfully, to the detriment of the overall project.

- To develop the goals and objectives. A goal is a description of the destination, and an objective is a measure of the progress needed to get to the destination. I have been on some projects in which you couldn't find a document that defined the goals of the project.

- Drive the desired behaviours, attitudes, and mindsets consistently. You need to role model the behaviours you want to form in the project culture. People will follow what you do and not what you say.

- Together with the team, define what success looks like and how it will be measured. Success is not just 'We delivered ahead of schedule and under budget' but should include the following aspects:

  » People and Culture

  » Expected Behaviour

  » Programme

  » Health and Safety

  » Quality

  » Environmental

- » Cost

- » Design

- » Stakeholder Engagement

- Sell the vision and goals of the project to the team, and gain buy-in from the team. The leader needs to be able to get team members to realise how their personal and career goals tie into the project's vision and goals. Brand the vision everywhere, and make it part of meeting start-ups. It should be known by everyone working on the project.

- Continuously inspire and motivate the team.

- Demonstrate strong preference for coaching rather than controlling the team.

- Empower the team, and help team members grow and develop new skills.

- Promote respect, trust, and safety.

- Create new leaders. A complex project requires several leaders to help motivate and keep the team engaged. The role of the project leader is to bring out the leadership in people and help them develop their leadership skills.

- Trust your team, and delegate decisions to the lowest level. This will ensure timely decision making on the project. The pace on a large infrastructure project is frenetic, and delays in decision making will result in cost and schedule overruns.

'Leadership is the art of getting someone else to do something you want done because he wants to do it.' — *Dwight D. Eisenhower*

For the project leader to be successful in executing their role and making their project successful, they need to be able to do the following right and continuously improve their skills:

- Communication

- Change your language

- Establish touchpoints

- Connect the project's vision to team member goals

- Establish roles and responsibilities for team members

- Keep team motivated

- Create a one-team mentality

- Keep their own motivation high

Communication

The project leader cannot fail to communicate. Even when you feel you are not communicating, you may actually be communicating the wrong things to your team.

'Communication is the real work of leadership.' — *Nitin Nohria*

Communication can be defined as the process of transmitting information and common understanding from one person to another (Keyton, 2011). It is the creation or exchange of thoughts, ideas, emotions, and understanding between sender(s) and receiver(s) (Dun 2002). This means that, as a leader, you are not just putting information out there. You have a responsibility to ensure that there is universal understanding between you and the recipients. This is not an easy thing for a project leader; it takes work to accomplish it. Any information you put out there also must have the underlying purpose of bringing the best out in people. Often, this is the part that is overlooked — what I will call 'communicating for the future'.

Benefits of Effective Communication

There are many benefits of communicating effectively:

- Creates job satisfaction — A project is constantly changing. It is natural for team members to want to know the leader's understanding of the status quo and whether they are undertaking their work as expected. Effective communication between the project leader and the team ensures that team members understand the overall direction of the job and whether they are performing as expected. This motivates the team and makes them feel like valued members. Effective communication helps build loyalty and trust, which contributes to a high-performance team.

- Gains top-level management support — Effective communication between the project leader and top-level management will ensure that they have what they want and understand the current status of the project and the actions being taken. This will reduce their urge to micromanage and will lead to support for the project leader's actions.

- Promotes stakeholder satisfaction — Effective communication with stakeholders will ensure they have the information they need and will make it easier for the leader to gain certain approvals. This is very important in permits and licensing, which usually involve government agencies.

- Results in fewer conflicts — Conflicts are easily resolved through effective communication and mutual discussions between team members and the leader. Fewer conflicts occur with your contractor when your communication is effective. This will save you cost and time on the project.

- Increases productivity — Effective communication means that your intended action is what is undertaken rather than what the team felt you wanted to be done. This will also ensure that actions are prompt, making better use of everyone's time.

- Helps in developing a high-performance team — An open and effective communication environment will create trust, increase productivity, and result in job satisfaction for team members. These are the critical ingredients in creating a high-performance team.

However, communication itself can be very complex. A simple written statement could have several meanings, depending on which words are stressed in the sentence. So, written communication can be dangerous and cause a lot of confusion on projects. However, due to the contractual nature of projects, written communication is the most widely used form of communication.

Face-to-face should be the preferred medium of communication, as you can read the body language of the people you are communicating with and gain immediate feedback. In projects, however, some communication needs to be recorded, especially when it is between the client and the contractor. Even in such cases, it is best to have a face-to-face discussion about the communication first, before putting it into writing. At the end of the day, the contractor's failure is your failure, and so you want to ensure at all times that your intended meaning is what the contractor receives.

Barriers to Communication

As George Bernard Shaw put it, *'The single biggest problem in communication is the illusion that it has taken place.'*

Your communication as a project leader may be with several stakeholders and your team, all of whom are in the room together and all of whom require different things. Your goal is to ensure that the intended meaning is what is received by removing 'noise' as much as possible. Noise could be language barriers, interruptions, emotions, etc. Individuals are more likely to perceive information favourably when it conforms to their own beliefs, values, and needs. In this day and age, when several cultures may be involved in a project, obtaining feedback is key to successful communication. I have been guilty of this several times in the past when I realised that something I communicated months ago was not understood in the context I meant it to be, introducing time risk into my project.

'To effectively communicate, we must realise that we are all different in the way we perceive the work and use this understanding as a guide to our communication with others.' — Anthony Robbins

There are four types of barriers to communication — or 'noise' — such as process barriers, physical barriers, semantic barriers, and psychosocial barriers (Eisenberg, 2010). The project leader should make every effort to remove the barriers to communication.

Process Barriers

Every step in the communication process is necessary to ensure the intended meaning is what is received. Any blocked steps become barriers.

> » *Sender Barriers* — A team member with a solution to a challenge fails to speak up in a meeting for fear of

criticism from others in the meeting. A project leader, when leading a meeting, should always be watching the body language of participants to ensure that they identify people wanting to offer ideas and give them the opportunity to speak. They should set the tone of meetings to ensure that everyone can contribute without the fear of being ridiculed. The idea that was ridiculed may very well save the project from entering into crisis. You can introduce meeting rules, which ensures everyone involved can speak up without fear of retribution.

» *Encoding Barriers* — A team member who is not fluent in the language being used may struggle to get his/her point across. In this case, patience and feedback are important to ensure that the message gets across as intended. Many projects now are multinational. And project leaders will need to be skilled at this.

» *Medium Barriers* — Emails are often the culprit in miscommunication. Sometimes it is better to have a face-face discussion first before sending an email if the issue is an emotional one.

» *Decoding Barriers* — The use of jargon and acronyms may sometimes result in the receiver not being able to interpret the message. The Rail and Nuclear industries are full of jargon that new entrants or stakeholders may not be conversant with. The project leader should always consider their audience when communicating.

» *Receiver Barriers* — Misconceptions the receiver has about the sender can easily distort the message received. We tend to evaluate or judge the information we receive based on our experience with that category of message. Bias and prejudice often play a part in miscommunication. It is important that, regardless of our experiences, we are open to ideas from everyone, even if that person has been untrustworthy in the past.

» *Feedback Barriers* — Failing to repeat communication back to people or failing to ask questions on understanding may cause you to miss the meaning that was intended.

Physical Barriers

In this modern day of leading projects, your team could be anywhere in the world. This presents a physical barrier of distance. This forces you to use other mediums of communication such as telephone calls and emails. However, modern-day technology also provides excellent video-conference capabilities, which need to be considered.

There are other physical barriers which people take for granted, but they can be overcome. Some examples: a telephone call whilst having a face-face conversation and people dropping in whilst you are in a communication. These physical barriers can be neutralised by making a conscious effort to turn phones off and set appointments for people.

Psychological and Social Barriers

Three important concepts associated with these are fields of experience, filtering, and psychological distance (Antos, 2011). When there is little overlap in people's experiences (biases, values, backgrounds, etc.), effective communication becomes an issue. Also, people are likely to filter what they are hearing to what they want to hear. Psychological distance can form between people who have previously fallen out on an issue. As a project leader, you need to be able to discuss contentious issues without getting emotional about them. There is a thin line between passion and being emotional about something and not letting it go.

Delivering and Receiving Communication

As I have mentioned, large infrastructure projects are made up of several stakeholders, teams, media exposure, and the requirement to make very quick decisions to improve the chances of success. The characteristics of large infrastructure projects mean that 'noise' is magnified, and one wrong communication could result in delays and significant cost increases. The following can serve as guidelines to increase the effectiveness of your communication.

When delivering the communication, consider:

- If you need to communicate this information. Is it going to create noise if you consider all the other communication going on?

- The true purpose of your communication. You need to identify the most important goal of your communication and then adapt your tone, language, and approach to ensure that goal is achieved.

- Clarifying your ideas before communicating. You need to analyse the idea and adequately plan it before communicating it.

- Consulting others first, if appropriate. Go to the extent of getting a second opinion of even your critical emails before sending them. Sometimes it may be good to write an important email, leave it for a day or two, and re-read it before sending. Whether it is written or oral communication, it is important to seek other opinions before communicating the information.

- Editing it critically and ensuring every word counts towards achieving your goal, whether it is verbal or written communication.

- The setting. Is this the right time to communicate this information although it may seem important?

- The overtones as well as the contents. Consider your tone of voice, expression, body language, and how receptive you are to the responses.

- Seeking feedback. Regardless of the medium, always seek feedback, and, in meetings, always summarise and confirm understanding.

- Do your attitude and actions confirm what you are communicating, not something else? People will interpret your actions and attitude more than your words.

- Communicating for the future not just for today. Consider the long-term goals that you want to achieve. On a project, you are interested in the overall behaviour and the working relationships with people. So, you have to take this into context whilst communicating.

When receiving the information:

- Listen for message content. You should try to hear exactly what the sender is saying in their message.

- Listen for feelings. You must always try to understand what the sender feels about the content of their message.

- Respond to feelings. The project leader should make the

sender aware that their feelings, as well as the message content, are being taken seriously.

- As we have explained, communication is both verbal and non-verbal, and the project leader should be listening for both. If the verbal cues conflict with the non-verbal cues, then you should seek to clarify what is being transmitted.

- Rephrase what has been communicated to you back to the sender. This will give the sender an opportunity to clarify their message if the intended meaning has not been received.

- Stop talking! You are not listening if you are talking at the same time, and that is not showing respect.

- Put the person talking at ease. Let the person feel that they can talk without being criticised and that you are prepared to act on the message.

- Look and act interested. Do not be on your phone or checking emails. This says, 'I do not have time for you'.

- Remove distractions. Go sit in a quiet place, if possible. Shut the meeting room door, and lock down the computer screen so that emails don't keep popping up and you're not tempted by that critical email you are waiting for.

- Empathise with the talker. Try to put yourself in the person's shoes to see the situation from their point of view.

- Be patient. Allow the person plenty of time to speak. If time is limited, book an appointment so the person knows the allocated time they have. We all understand that projects are busy places and that there is not a lot of time for project leaders to chat. However, you can book an appointment and inform the person of the time available to you so they can prepare and know you have the time for him/her.

Effective communication is easy to talk about, write about, and teach, but not easy to practise. However, by making a conscious effort to apply and reflect on your mistakes on a daily basis, one will improve. Our ability to communicate effectively stems from respect. If you respect someone, you are likely to give the person a chance. Know that you do not know everything there is to know in life and that someone may just say something that may make a significant difference in a project. This will help you respect the person, which tends to ensure more effective communication.

Stalin, Churchill, and Roosevelt, during World War II, believed that the right communication could shape reality. This was the reason for many of their speeches at the time of a hard-fought war.

Therefore, in time of great difficulty, the leader's ability to communicate to shape their people's mentality will ultimately lead to the success of the project.

Thus, a project leader should, therefore, take their communication very seriously. A project is a battle or war against unknown risks and sometimes Mother Nature. A project leader's ability to communicate unambiguously during ever-changing scenarios will determine whether the project is successful or not.

Communication methods will vary for individuals on the project team. The project leader should be able to establish which form of communication works best for people and adapt their communication style to suit. Individuals learn from a variety of methods: visual, auditory, reading, and kinetic. I prefer brainstorming and drawing on boards, as that makes me communicate better or take information in better. What is yours?

Change Your Language

'In the beginning was the Word, and the Word was with God, and the Word was God.'

'Through Him, all things were made, and without Him, nothing was made that has been made.'

I am a Christian. I operate from and wholeheartedly try to live according to those words. However, even if you are not a Christian, you should understand that words have a creative force behind them. What we say shapes our world! In fact, what all the motivational and 'laws of attraction' speakers are trying to get you to do is one thing: Create your world with your words. We say 'We are what we eat'; however, the even scarier thing is 'We are what we say'!

We also are attracted to and pushed toward what we talk about the most. The words we speak create and shape our ideas and that of our team. Out of our ideas come our beliefs. If we keep on speaking in a particular way and this informs the beliefs of the team and our own, then we have already created the force that will determine whether we succeed or fail. We cannot achieve beyond our belief system. Therefore, the belief system you create in your team will shape whether you will achieve your goals or not.

One view holds that our words express our thoughts and affirm to people how we see ourselves, think about the world, or see things. But our thoughts are fed by our words, which shape our thoughts. The things we speak to people also shape their thoughts and how they see things and, therefore, create the world around us.

If the words we speak create our thoughts, our belief system, our attitudes, and our world, then we need to make a conscious effort to **change our language!**

Words like 'we can't', 'we won't', 'problem', and all negative words should be removed from a project leader's vocabulary. The word 'challenge' can be substituted for 'problem' because challenge conveys the notion of something that brings the best in you. Better still is the word 'opportunity' for 'problem' or 'challenge'. That is, everything is an opportunity to be exploited, and you just need to develop that mindset to enable you to see the opportunities. Also, rather than using the phrase 'it is your fault', a better phrase is 'it is your responsibility'. The project leader's words and communications should focus on creating a positive mentality and a can-do attitude in the team.

I recall hearing some project leaders making fun of their own programme deadlines — that they were unachievable and that there was no way the programme could achieve those objectives. I was shocked that someone being paid to bring a project in on time and budget was making such statements! No wonder their packages came in way over budget and extremely late. If you, the project leader, don't believe your goals, then how are you going to get buy-in from your team and the contractor? In this scenario, it becomes a self-fulfilling prophecy. You don't believe it anyway, so you don't put in the effort to achieve the goal.

The project leader should be very cautious of every word they use and make their words count in creating the attitude, atmosphere, and the belief system about the project and its chances for success. This will not be easy and will require constant practice, reminding yourself and assigning people to make you accountable for the words you use.

Touchpoints

The world is currently full of technology intended to make us more effective. But does it, or does it just make us 'busy'? On a project, there are many decisions to be made. Some are big, and others may not look significant at the time. The point is that there are constant demands on the project leader's time. Project leaders are constantly being interrupted whether in the middle of a critical email or report or during their lunch times. Project leader's diaries can become untenable as people go in, look for time, and book appointments to enable the leader to help them with an issue. And some people will pop over to ask a question. In today's era of open-plan offices, this opens the opportunity for your team to interact with you at any time.

And so, in the setting of this busy environment, your design manager pops over to your desk and wants to give you feedback on a workshop they had last week when you are in the middle of a critical email. What do you do? Send them away or talk to them whilst you type the critical email? As a project leader, you will be faced with several of these decisions on a daily basis. You will hear project leaders say that they are now doing their work after hours, after dealing with everyone's issues. And what that means is writing a critical report or checking their emails. Is that truly the way a project leader should be working?

As a project leader, you can view these interactions as distractions and do other people's work, or you can view them as opportunities. For you to be able to view these interactions in a positive light, you need to remind yourself of your role as the project leader. Your role includes creating the vision, getting buy-in for the vision, empowering the team, creating the right attitude and belief system in the team, and, in so doing, creating a high-performance team.

To be able to perform our role effectively, we need these interactions. We must commit to making them count and reach a positive outcome. Your goal is to ensure that any interaction you have with anyone creates an environment that will lead to high performance. The positive interactions that lead to high performance are what is called Touchpoints.

Both bad and good news spreads like wildfire by people relaying it to others. On the average, bad experiences are relayed to a minimum of 10-11 people. Your interactions with a team member, if it inspires and motivates them, will be relayed to 2 or 3 people. They will, in turn, relate it to others, and your influence circle starts to grow. If your interactions are positive, others coming to you will be open to your ideas, and you will face less resistance when sharing new ideas.

As a project leader, a number of these interactions may come as a surprise. You need to prepare and plan for these interactions. Whatever interaction with whomever at whichever place should be something you walk away from knowing that you had a positive impact on the situation.

When these interactions come to you as a surprise, welcome them, and practise all the active-listening skills and effective communication that we have discussed in this chapter. On the rare occasion that you really need to complete something you are working on, be courteous to ask the person how long it will take. If it cannot be accommodated, reschedule a time to discuss it. However, remember that your role as a leader is to serve, not to be served, and you should make the time. If these interactions are positive and they empower the team, leading to high performance, there will come a time when you won't have as many interruptions. You will begin to seek them out to maintain the progress or take it to the next level.

Making all these interactions positive is not easy and requires continuous practice and daily reflection on how your interactions went. After reflection, if you believe the interactions did not go as planned, make an effort to correct this by initiating more positive interactions with the individuals concerned.

'Leadership is about making others better as a result of your presence and making sure that impact lasts in your absence.' — Sheryl Sandberg

Connecting Project Vision to Team Member's Goals

We all know that having a vision is a critical success factor for everything in life and even more so for large infrastructure projects, where changes can be fast and significant. However, it is not often that team members on projects can tell you what the vision of a project is. At times, a vision statement may exist, but it may be hidden in an obscure document that most people are not aware of. A vision that no one knows about is really no vision. If the team is not aware of the project's vision, then the leadership is failing. This is because a leader's role is to create the vision and the environment and to motivate and inspire the team to achieve that vision.

There is a biblical statement that says, 'Where there is no vision, the people perish'. It also applies to projects: 'Where there is no vision, the project fails'.

The first thing is to create the vision. The next critical thing is to *connect* the project vision to team member's goals. To be able to do this the vision statement should be inspiring, mean something, and bring out emotions in people.

A good project vision statement should have the following:

- The vision statement should go beyond the project's technical and financial agenda. It should seek to leave a positive legacy on the people and communities it impacts. Large infrastructure projects form part of a bigger government agenda, like producing green energy and reducing the reliance on fossil fuel, thereby preserving the earth. They are also built to provide transport links from the local community to other areas, thereby making the world a global village.

- Your vision statement should be short, punchy, and memorable. Background information can be provided in a separate document. This short, punchy, inspiring version should be communicated across all media to keep the project team connected to it.

- It should be written in the present and not future tense. It should describe what the team will feel, think, say, and do as if they have already achieved the vision.

- It should describe an outcome — the best outcome the project can achieve. It shouldn't confuse vision with the project goal and objectives for a particular period of time. A vision statement should not provide numeric measures of success and also not be a generic statement applicable to every project or business.

- It shouldn't use language that is open to interpretation — like business-speak or words like 'maximise' or 'minimise'.

- It should be kept simple for people in the project and outside the project. It should be kept free of industry and technical jargons and buzzwords.

- Emotions are a powerful thing, and the vision should invoke emotions in people. Passion is everything, and the vision should be a passionate cry! However, it should separate the 'hard' aspect of vision — what we see, hear, and do — from the 'soft' aspect of vision — what we think and feel.

- It should help build a picture, the same picture, in people's minds.

- It needs to align with the values and culture you want exhibited on the project.

Spend time on workshops to come up with an inspiring, passionate vision which invokes certain values and culture in the team. As with everything, there is a lot of help on the Internet. Research some of the best visions, and draft one to suit your project's values and objectives.

An example of a good vision statement is that of Amazon:

'Our vision is to be earth's most customer-centric company, to build a place where people can come to find and discover anything they might want to buy online.' (Quoted from Amazon.com)

After you have come up with a fantastic vision, you need to make it come alive on the project and make it real and on everyone's lips. You need to be discussing the vision at meetings and making it visual, so it is ingrained in the team. One of the best ways to help the team deliver the project vision is to link their yearly goals to the project's vision. Most goals on projects are tied to programme and cost-efficiency objectives. These are great, but if your vision is to create 'a world-class project', then simply tying team goals to just programme and cost efficiencies may not be good enough or a little short-sighted. You will need to define what you mean by your vision and create objectives for the team that lead to attaining that vision. Assuming your vision is to create a world-class project, then, of course, programme and cost efficiencies may be part of those goals. But there should be higher goals, like building an excellent team. Creating that exemplary team comes with behaviours, values, and a culture which you will need to promote.

One of the reasons the construction of the London Olympic Games infrastructure was successful was that they had a clear vision. Sir John Armitt, CBE, chairman of National Express and the former chairman of London's Olympic Delivery Authority (ODA) for the 2012 Games, said that the entire project had a number of key objectives. The first was that it was to be the 'greenest' games ever, which was an enormous challenge. Considering that the site — the new Queen Victoria Park — was highly contaminated. This drove several of their decisions.

The takeaway should be this: Don't write your vision for the project only to tick the box and then forget about it. You need to ensure that the team is working towards this vision actively. The best way to do this is to connect all your yearly and six-month goals to your project's overall vision.

Roles and Responsibilities of the Team Members

Everyone knows that roles and responsibilities are another critical success factor for large infrastructure projects. But is this a reality on your project — or do you only have a generic job description you received whilst being recruited? You join a project, and you are not really clear on how you contribute to the bigger picture and other things that push the project towards its vision. Have you ever felt this way? I have, and I know countless other people who have experienced the same as well. You will hear people say, 'Make yourself useful' or 'Let's just get on with it'. These are all great attitudes for can-do people, but it is not an efficient way of delivering a project. On large infrastructure projects, this can lead to duplication of effort and unnecessary bottlenecks in information flow. This can also lead to unnecessary competition among team members, who feel they need to out-do their fellow team members, resulting in a back-biting culture — a recipe for disaster.

As a project leader, your expectations for your team members should be clear.

Without a roles-and-responsibilities matrix, team members can become confused about who is doing what, attending what meetings, supporting which initiatives, what reports are expected of them, etc. This may seem minor, but it is critical for creating a high-performance team.

A roles-and-responsibilities matrix should be written and circulated among the team, so team members know who to contact on particular issues and who is doing what. This is not a generic document that says what is expected of project managers, etc. Those documents have their place, but you will need a bit more detail in a team.

On large infrastructure projects, thousands of people will be employed. The project leader will not be able to develop all this by himself. My advice is that you develop this for your direct reports, and they develop this for their direct reports, till it gets to package leaders of sizes 40 or less who develop it for their teams. The package leader will also have direct reports, and they will also need to develop further details for their respective teams. In this manner, every one of the team members will know exactly what is expected of them and how they contribute to the overall project vision.

You should conduct a survey. If it comes out that people are not clear on what they are doing or what others are doing, then it is not just an organisational chart that they need but a detailed roles-and-responsibilities matrix.

Keeping Teams Motivated

The leader's role is to keep the energy in the team up and keep the team motivated to achieve the vision and goals of the project. Due to the long durations of large-infrastructure projects, this is a tough job — but it is critical to ensure its success. Some people think that motivation is something that just pumps people up but doesn't do much else. However, motivation can be the leader's number-one asset on large infrastructure projects, with their many highs and lows.

To achieve anything on a project, your team must be willing to put all their energy into achieving the project goals rather their own personal agendas. It is the responsibility of the project leader to understand what motivates their team so that they can bring the best out of them.

Vroom (1994) stated that the performance of your employees is based on four factors:

- **Performance** — how well the work is performed

- **Environment** — the context in which the task is to be performed

- **Ability** — the skills and knowledge to perform the task well

- **Motivation** — the incentive to perform the task well

Thus, the project leader's goal is to ensure that the team has the resources and the right skills required to do their tasks. They must create the right environment for the team, and then they have to continuously motivate the team to commit themselves to achieving the project goals.

What Is Motivation?

Rogers (2004) proposed that all humans have a driving force that stimulates them to achieve goals which are prompted by comparison of the concepts of 'self' and 'ideal self'. Everyone has an ideal person in their mind in terms of abilities, strengths, and status that they believe they can achieve which is different from their current self. The goal for the leader is to create the environment that helps the team members to identify how the work they are doing helps them to get closer to their ideal self.

What Motivates Us?

Most people feel that money is the greatest motivator, but research has confirmed that, once you are earning a certain amount of income, money no longer motivates you. If an individual feels they are paid the right amount of money, then adding more to their salary may look good but will not necessarily motivate the person. Every human being wants to be respected, challenged, and recognised for their effort. They want to know that what he or she is doing is contributing to a greater good and even to the betterment of humanity.

The 'Topos de Tlatelolco', meaning 'Tlatelolco Moles' demonstrates how contributing to a greater good tends to motivate teams greatly when their basic needs are met. This group, which was formed in February 1986 after a serious earthquake in Mexico, works for free to support government services. This voluntary search-and-rescue group will enter places that paid employees are afraid to enter to rescue someone. What is their motivation? To contribute to the greater good by saving lives.

Taking these into consideration, the following are some of the ways to keep the team constantly motivated:

- Let everyone on the team feel they are helping deliver the overall project vision. This means there can be no 'over-selling' of the vision. Let the security personnel know they are helping to build a green energy project that will help in climate change, if that is the vision for your project.

- Pay the right salary. I started by stating that money is not a motivator if you are paid right. You should not try to save the project money by paying people below industry standards or what you think they deserve. Once you pay an individual the right salary, their focus is no longer on how much they earn but on delivering results.

- Enjoy the journey. Don't wait till there is a big milestone before celebrating. Delivering a project is a journey every-one is on together. Ensure that your team enjoys the jour-ney by organising team events that involve everyone — and make it more than just going out for meals. Organise sporting activities that involve teams. The Network Rail Western and Wales region in the United Kingdom used to organise sporting days which involved tug-of-war con-tests. How the tug-of-war was won became points of dis-cussion on what the team mechanism is and how work-ing together can create success.

- Celebrate milestones. Break the project up into major and minor milestones, and celebrate when you achieve them. Major milestones could be celebrated with badges, mugs, etc. The Hinkley Point C project in the United Kingdom used to celebrate this with nicely crafted badges, which made people proud.

- Openly celebrate individuals. Congratulating others openly — in front of others — for their great work is a great way to boost morale and motivate. This doesn't need to be a special award ceremony. Just speaking well about people's performance when they least expect it is a big motivator. Thanking people for their great work with seniors copied in is a huge motivator.

- Communicate, communicate, communicate. Nothing de-motivates like a team who don't know what is going on. You need to have one-on-ones, group meetings, etc., to keep people informed on what is going on. The project should have newsletters and briefing sessions to ensure that the team are up to speed. This should not be just at the high, senior levels. It should be replicated in package leader's teams as well. Some projects use a board briefing every Monday morning, where they all get together, brief each other, and give people the opportunity to ask questions and clarify issues. My advice is to combine all the forms of communicating with your team according to the size of the team.

- Involve people. People want to be involved in coming up with solutions. If they are involved, buy-in is quicker, and there are fewer conflicts.

- Set challenging goals. The human mind feels more accomplished when it overcomes a challenging goal. After achieving a stretched target, the team is pumped up and want to take on the next challenge. The motivation and energy gained from overcoming a stretched target should always be channelled immediately into the next target. Goals should be realistic; otherwise, the team will be demotivated. One of the ways to keep the energy up and team motivated at all times is to mix stretched targets with ones that are not so stretched. This allows time for the team to recuperate and keep the momentum going with the knowledge that they are hitting the targets. When a target is missed, don't dwell too much on the failure; assess it, learn the lessons, focus on the positives, and quickly move on.

- Give people the resources they need to succeed. No one is superman! If people don't have the right resources to operate, they will soon become frustrated and demotivated.

- Inspire and persuade through empathy and trust — not through your positional power. The new generation does not work well in the face of intimidation.

- Manage poor performance. People want to know they are doing well. If they are not doing so well, then they need to be guided to improve. Also, rather than brushing underperformance under the carpet, you need to address it. Poor performance demotivates others as well.

- Lead by example. Do what you said you would do. If people realise you do what you say and say what you mean, they will follow suit and feel motivated.

- Care about the individuals in your team. Don't give the impression that you are just about goals! You need to show a passion for the development of your team members. What are their life goals? Is there something you can do —whether by coaching, assigning different types of work, or keeping in contact — that will help enable them to achieve their life goals? If a team realises that their leader cares about them — and not just hitting project milestones — they are likely to respond in kind and feel motivated.

- Ask only for the things you really need. Have you ever had a manager who asked you to drop the critical things you are doing to produce a deliverable — but fails afterwards to even review the deliverable? Later, they realise what you told them was critical was really what was critical. How did you feel? Did your motivation drop as you lost confidence in the manager? If you do the same, your team members will lose confidence in you, too.

- Ensure that there are deputies for your team so that the leaders can recuperate and recharge their batteries.

- The leader must continue to evolve, adapt, and adjust to external changes to prevent the energy in the team from dropping.

As Peter Drucker has pointed out, the chief objective of leadership is the creation of a human community held together by the bond of working toward a common purpose.

Creating a One-Team Mentality

Often, the construction team wants to prove that they are better than the project-management team, the commercial team wants everyone to know they control the project, the client team thinks they can deliver the project better than the contractor, the client team thinks they don't need the delivery partner, etc.! It is easy for people to forget that they are working together to build a project successfully. Who cares whether the construction team or the project-management team or the commercial team or the delivery partner is the reason for the success of the project? All anyone should care about is that the project was a huge success. However, if the project fails, the project leader is to blame! People create a victim mentality that says the project failed because the contractor or construction team were not good enough. As a project leader, the success of the project is your responsibility — you are accountable for all decisions. All risks, regardless of your contractual mechanism, are client risks.

If you have everyone pulling in different directions, then it will be a frustrating journey that will not lead to success. You need to develop a 'one-team' mentality and understand that 'if one fails, then we all fail'. It is your role to ensure everyone on the project, including all suppliers and stakeholders, are successful.

In developing a 'one-team' mentality, clients need to understand that suppliers/contractors are not charity organisations. Their needs in the project also should be met.

We have all been on projects where we had to put our career on the line to force a 'one-team' mentality. This always pays off, and great results are achieved. This can work so well that people will forget who is responsible and chip in to support when others are struggling. Develop an attitude of 'the best man for the job regardless of who is responsible'. This does not mean that you accept underperformance but that you all strive towards the same goal.

The following are some of the things you should do to develop a 'one-team' mentality:

- Lead by example. The success of the project should be your number-one priority — over even your career. This may sound odd, but if you play politics to safeguard your career rather than focus on the success of the project, you will be found out one day, which *will* derail your career. Don't be short-sighted and focus only on the short term. Think of all the success all your projects will bring you one day. You must demonstrate the 'one-team' mentality and lead from the front. Remember: you create the attitude of the project environment.

- Agree on what 'combined success' means. The contractor and client all have different definitions of success, and so do all the stakeholders involved on the project. Run workshops with all stakeholders and agree what success looks like and means. Get every stakeholder involved, and let everyone's voice be heard. Don't feel obligated to accept a client's definition of success just because they are paying the bills. The same attitude should prevail with the project manager's definition of success: It should not be accepted as the only definition of success without listening to the construction team, environmental team, delivery partner, or whoever the stakeholders may be.

- Develop the emotional intellect of the team. If each stakeholder can look at success from the other's point of view, they are more likely to agree and work together.

- Force a language change. Encourage the team to stop using the word 'they' and to start using the word 'we'. If a team member comes over and says 'they' haven't met a milestone, correct it to 'we haven't met a milestone'. Your next question should be 'What have we done to help achieve the milestone?' This kind of simple language change forces people to be more accountable.

- Drum the 'one fails, all fail' mentality. Make people understand that, regardless of what they feel, if one stakeholder fails, then we all have failed. Ban all 'victim mentality' culture. This will force people to support, hold people accountable, and be more proactive rather than passive.

- It is the threat of being left out that exacerbates ego problems and creates clashes. The leader must ensure that they don't create an environment that invites ego contests.

- Encourage the team to help create an environment in which each team member will be successful with their duties.

- Never reward passive onlookers. Don't reward people who sit back and wait for another stakeholder to fail. Make them accountable for the failure as well if they could have helped in any way.

Project Leadership — Keeping Your Own Motivation High

Project leadership can be really tough because the project leader must shield their team from whatever surprises come up. Project leaders must be reliable, should always be there to support their team under all conditions, should have integrity, and honour their words and promises.

When it seems the whole world is hanging on your shoulders, it can sap your energy level and motivation. On a major project, many things can pose simultaneous challenges: a lack of motivation, budget issues, programme pressures, and people's behaviour. At times, it will seem like everyone is coming to you with their challenges, and all you seem to do is to give and give. This can result in a lack of motivation, a feeling of being overwhelmed and tired, and sometimes even depression. This is where being passionate about what you do can be a blessing and a curse at the same time. It is a blessing because you will be proactively looking for ways to overcome the challenges. However, it can also be a curse when it makes you feel like you need to do it alone and do not employ the right tools, causing you to get stressed.

To keep your team members motivated, encourage them to have a 'best friend' at work so that they can work through issues together. For project leaders, it is sometimes not that easy, as you are seen as the rock of the project, which makes it difficult to confide in people about your fears. The ability to keep yourself motivated is not a one-size-fits-all, as everyone responds to challenges differently.

The following are some of the tools and strategies that will help keep your motivation levels up:

- For you to excel at anything, you should be in a career that you are passionate about. You should be able to link your career goals to your life goals if they are different. The project you are working on should contribute to your career goals, which relate to your life goals. At times of stress on a project, you should always remind yourself of why you are doing what you are doing. That is, your focus should be on your vision for your life. This will enable you to work through stressful times and increase your motivational energy.

- Ensure that you have a support system at home. Your spouse and close family members can be a good support system. At times, you just need someone on whom you can vent your frustration and display some weakness without being judged. Some friends can also be a great support structure; however, choose them wisely in this age of the rat race, where everyone wants to get ahead of everyone else.

- Be positive, and remember that nothing in this world is permanent, including difficult times. Continuously remind yourself that this challenge will pass away and that the future will be brighter. If you can have a mindset that challenges are not permanent and that their only purpose is to make us stronger and improve our skills, you will feel energised.

- Remember your past wins over other challenges in life, and draw energy and motivation from them.

- Watch motivational videos. There are many on the Internet.

- Remember that there is nothing new under the sun and that solutions to the challenges you are facing may just be a click away on the Internet.

- If you have faith, use it. I am a Christian, and I rely on prayer as my number-one stress buster.

- Religiously draw up the 5 top critical things that will make a difference in the project and focus on these. In this case, you don't need any 'nice-to-haves'. Focus on the critical ones, the failure of which could lead to crisis on the project.

- If you don't already have one, find a mentor outside your organisation who is experienced in your area of work to bounce ideas off and seek advice from.

- Consider using the services of a coach; sometimes you have the answers within you, and all you need to do is to talk to someone who will coax it out of you.

- Use the gym. Sometimes you need the diversion to get you relaxed so you can perform better at work. Also, exercise produces endorphins (natural painkillers in your brain); this will reduce stress, help you to sleep better, and improve your motivational energy.

- Have some 'me' time during the week when you do absolutely nothing — no distractions, including phones, TV, kids, spouse, work, etc. — just 30 minutes to an hour for yourself when you do nothing. Many inventions have come from 'me time', and some of the answers to your challenges may present themselves during this time.

Leadership in any capacity is tough. Project leadership in large infrastructure projects is *really* tough because money influences behaviour — something a project leader must grapple with on a daily basis. However, it is rewarding when you get it right. The goal is to be better every day than you were the day before, reflecting on each day, and pushing towards achieving mastery.

As a project leader, you might be pulled down by politics, do something dumb, make a bad decision, or just wear out. The only school for real leaders is challenges and how you respond to them. As Warren Bennis wrote in his book *On Becoming a Leader*, 'Leaders learn by leading, and they learn best by leading in the face of obstacles. As weather shapes the mountains, so problems make leaders. Difficult bosses, lack of vision and virtue in the executive suite, circumstances beyond their control, and their own mistakes have been the leader's 'basic curriculum'.

Embrace every difficulty with the knowledge that it will make you better. This attitude will serve as your best motivation.

To sum this chapter up, Max De Pree, in *Leadership is an Art*, wrote, 'The first responsibility of a leader is to define reality. The last is to say "Thank you". In between, the leader is a servant'.

Chapter 12:

Case Studies

In this chapter, I discuss some studies of projects I was involved in and also have researched and how some of the topics discussed in this book were utilised, the challenges faced, and how successful they were.

In all the projects, not every critical success factor I have discussed were fully employed, so I will focus on which ones were employed successfully, and the lessons learnt that highlight the need for the critical success factors.

I will not be discussing costs, as that kind of information is confidential.

Reading Elevated Railway and Feeder Line Work

This package of work was a critical part of the Reading Station Area Redevelopment Project, which is seen as one of Network Rail's very successful projects.

The Elevated Railway was required to grade separate the fast lines from the slow lines at Reading to remove a known bottleneck at the station. This project was reported on extensively and also featured in *Rail Engineer* April 2014 Issue114 as 'The Last Piece of the Jigsaw'. It consisted of a 2km viaduct for the High-Speed line, a 1km viaduct for the cross-country lines, and a new freight line.

The project was complex, with some sections of the construction being undertaken 2 metres away from live rail and some over live rail. It was a Build Only contract, using ICE 7th edition contract.

Some of the reasons for the project's success were:

1. Top-level management support.

    The project managers on the project had extreme top-level management support from leaders Bill Henry, who was the project director, and Robbie Burns, who was the Western and Wales regional director. They supported the project managers in their decisions and believed they had hired the right people to deliver the project. Even at a time when the tier 1 contractor claimed the client's project managers were not supportive, the senior leaders supported their project managers and involved the seniors of the tier 1 contractor, which led to a reshuffling of their senior team. The two teams' (client and tier 1) contractor later bonded together and drove the project to success.

2. Making the procurement process count.

    The tender questions identified the complex areas of the project for the contractors to seek solutions to. The project did not pick standard questions for the contractor. The questions were specific on things that were necessary for the contractor to spend time on which would help the contractor be successful. There were site visits showing the contractors the complex areas of the project, which were discussed onsite. The contractor was given almost twice as long as other similar projects for them to return their tender responses. It involved presentations and discussions on the complex area of the work. The feedback from the contractors tendering for the contract was that this was the best they had seen in the industry and that the client demonstrated in-depth knowledge of the work.

3. Developing a robust project schedule.

   The client understood the schedule that was required to build the project and had planned all the interfaces and possessions required and booked all of this in advance of the work. Accepting the schedule for the project involved several deep dives to ensure that the complex areas were properly looked at and accounted for.

4. Monitoring and control.

   The Schedule Performance Index was religiously monitored and used to make critical decisions on the project. The project used concrete skylines — histograms of how much concrete was required to be poured weekly — to understand what actions needed to be done. The contractor went through a daily ritual of assessing what had been achieved and reviewed how it could be made better and how productivity could be improved.

5. Proactive risk management.

   Risk management was very proactive on this project. At one point, the client, through their risk management, realised that certain critical services which were required to be diverted by the contractor were better managed by the client. The client took this on board and diverted the services so that the contractor could focus on other aspects of the work. Proactive risk management meant that the client could bring their other contractors in to support certain aspects of the work, which were mitigation plans to identified risks.

6. Reactive troubleshooting.

    As mentioned, projects sometimes do fall into crisis, no matter how they are planned. A tender underbid which was later corrected initially raised a number of issues, causing the programme to run several months behind schedule. We were initially told that it was not statistically possible to turn the project around and hit the project milestones. A team was put together that went through deep dives and identified the issues with the project. It was initially a mini-tiger team; however, the project leaders realised the team was in control of this and let them get on with it, reporting to a steering group on progress. One of the solutions was changing the contract and including incentive milestones to help people focus on the milestones. The others were changing the client-contractor relationships and working more closely together, better defining roles and responsibilities for the client staff, and a change in mentality to win-win. The project went ahead and hit all its milestones.

7. Project leadership.

    Leadership — from the Western and Wales through to the project directors on Reading — was excellent. This went through to the various packages, including the Elevated Railway package. There were sporting events for the entire Western and Wales teams. BBQs were held for contractors on the Reading Station Area Redevelopment Projects. Hitting milestones was celebrated extensively — and in style — on the Elevated Railway project, for both contractor and client.

There was a 'one-team' mentality, which was reported in the Rail Engineer Magazine. There were no differences between client and contractor. The two were working to achieve the milestones, and that was all that mattered. The drive to hit goals was so evident that there was a buzz in the team. The concrete supplier once had their plant flooded. The contractor sent their pumps to the concrete supplier to pump out the water to get the machine started so that they could supply the weekly concrete. This is how dedicated the team were to meeting milestones.

Development of the team was a collective enterprise. Client project managers supported anyone who wanted to develop their skills towards professional qualifications. There was a coach on board who was available to support anyone who wanted to develop their leadership skills.

This was a project on which everyone who worked and left was later proud they had worked on such a project. Some believed that the manner in which the client and contractor worked together might never happen again. However, there are several projects around the world achieving the same success.

Reading West Curve Bridge Replacement Work

This bridge replacement work was a fantastic engineering project. It is on the Internet as part of the Reading Station Area Redevelopment Project. The project involved replacing an existing brick arch bridge with a concrete portal bridge.

The concrete portal bridge was constructed offsite, and, within a 101-hour railway possession, the rail track was removed, the arch bridge demolished, a new foundation installed, the portal bridge moved in with self-propelled modular transport, and the tracks re-installed.

1.   Developing a robust schedule.

Like most of Network Rail's critical rail-possession projects, these are planned years out with a good understanding of how the work will be constructed and possessions applied for. At a year out (T-52 weeks), Network Rail delivering work in possession kicks in, and all resources and access are booked. This is a rigid planning procedure that Network Rail adopted in 2009 after possession overruns at Shields Junction, Liverpool Street, and Rugby over the Christmas 2007 period had a major financial and reputational impact on Network Rail.

Six months before the starting day, we got all the subcontractors, including the designer, in a room and went through the schedule for the 101-hr possession work in detail. This highlighted several risks to the schedule that we needed to consider. One of the risks identified was the ability to obtain concrete for the foundation during Christmas and ensuring we had no issue with the time required for it to set. We mitigated this risk by changing the foundation from concrete to 75mm stones.

The work involved installing sheet piles to hold the earth cutting back whilst we dug the foundations. To ensure that we allowed adequate time for this, we undertook trial pile installations next to the bridge to understand how long we needed to allow for the piling operations.

Through these scheduled deep dives with all the subcontractors, we identified work that was not critical to be completed during the possession work and highlighted them as potential drop-outs if we were struggling with time. We considered risks of things that could go wrong and wrote mitigation plans for these.

The schedule was run through, with each subcontractor present going through their process and agreeing on their contingency measures.

2. Reactive troubleshooting.

We believed we had planned for everything and had backup equipment for everything.

The work involved digging into competent ground. However, during the night, we went past the depth at which competent ground was to be found as indicated by the designer. We called the lead engineer in, who took samples, undertook calculations during the possession, and gave a new depth to dig to.

Two days into the possession work, we were 17 hours behind. This meant constant review and re-planning of the work and implementing some of the mitigation measures we had identified during our deep dives. Some mitigation measures we had to improvise on and come up with new ones during the night. We completed the project on time with no delay to the network. This project went on to win several awards and was a finalist in the British Construction Industry Awards.

Crossrail

The Crossrail project involved construction of a 118km railway running through parts of London Berkshire, Buckinghamshire, and Essex. The project, which had a budget circa £15.9bn, was the largest infrastructure project in Europe prior to the start of the High Speed

2 project, also in the United Kingdom. The work included approximately 42km of tunnels, nine number new stations, and several other infrastructures. Below are lessons learnt; the information comes from the Crossrail Learning Legacy website.

1. Supplier collaboration.

   Crossrail Limited states they achieved 54% performance improvement through supplier collaboration.

2. Proactive risk management.

   The key Lessons and Recommendations from the project:

   - Risk management should be seen as a collaborative process, utilising the skills and expertise of all parties to manage and mitigate risk.

   - Risks should be owned by the organisation most able to manage the risk. This should be clearly documented in the contractual information.

   - The approach to risk management should align with the delivery model and be supported by clear policies, processes, procedures, and systems to enable consistency.

   - Process maturity reviews should be used to drive performance through collaboration and knowledge sharing.

   The initial budget was £15.9bn. As a result of value engineering and risk mitigation, Crossrail was able to retire £1.1bn of the funding package in 2010, leaving a revised budget of £14.8bn.

3. Monitoring and control.

   - Earned Value and Earned Schedule were critical parts of the monitoring of the Crossrail project.

   - Milestone tracking and critical-path analysis were also key to the project.

   - Crossrail had robust interface management and control procedures.

4. Project leadership.

   Crossrail's vision of 'A world-class, affordable railway delivered through effective partnerships and project excellence' would be delivered through best practices and responsible procurement. The vision was embedded into procurement strategies that retained the services of a project delivery partner, a programme partner, designers, and contractors. The vision was also embedded into development agreements, with key stakeholders that would contribute to the scheme, including London Underground, Network Rail, Canary Wharf Group, and Berkeley Homes.

   Crossrail ensured that their vision was what drove the project in every aspect. To ensure this happened, they developed a document titled 'Delivering Crossrail through Best Practice and Responsible Procurement' in December 2017. This document summarised the sponsorship and ownership for delivery of the project, how it would be governed, the basic programme and strategy for construction of the tunnels, and how the project would be organised for delivery. All these principles, including procurement and technical assurance, were translated into briefing material that formed part of the tender requirements for contracts for the project delivery and programme partners.

In 2012 Crossrail refined their vision to 'Moving London Forward'. This, together with their mission of delivering a world-class railway that fast-tracks the progress of London, brought together several organisations around a common goal and set of values: safety, inspiration, respect, collaboration, and integrity. These values, which were important to Crossrail, drove the behaviours necessary to achieve the project's objectives to be world class, safe, on time, and within funding.

One of the most admirable things you can see from the Crossrail success was the importance of leadership, vision, and a set of values in driving the behaviours through the project and supply chain.

Channel Deepening Project, Victoria, Australia

The Channel Deepening Project, whose estimated project cost in the final Business Case was $969m, was one of the largest and most critical maritime projects ever undertaken in Victoria. The project involved dredging 22 million cubic metres of sand and silt from existing channels.

The project was completed one month ahead of schedule and $200m below the estimated budget in the Business Case.

The following are the success factors on this project that I feel align with the concepts in this book:

- There was strong support by the government. The project leader had very strong top-level management support.

- Risk Analysis — They implemented robust risk management and mitigation processes.

- The project was an alliance project, which meant the levels of collaboration on the project were very high. However, the critical point here was that the culture, values, and commitments of the parties made it a success.

- It goes without saying that they had a robust estimate from the start.

Northern Expressway, South Australia

The project, which cost $564m, was the largest road construction project undertaken in South Australia since the 1960s. The project involved construction of 23km of a four-lane road with an associated cycle and pedestrian path linking the Gawler Bypass with Port Wakefield Road. The project was a design-and-construct contract. The project was delivered three months ahead of schedule and within the budget set. The completion date for this project had already been brought forward by a year, and, so, this was a significant achievement.

Some of the key project insights from *Infrastructure Planning and Delivery: Best Practice Case Studies* (December 2010):

- 'Attention to the risks associated with the Northern Expressway project and the most cost-effective strategies for dealing with individual risks was an important part of the scoping, planning, and procurement phases of the project'.

- 'A team culture supporting collaboration and co-ownership of issues had to be created by the project leadership team. The project director's focus on the value of teams and the importance of team development played a key role in the development of this culture, as did ensuring that the integrated project-management team was the right size (despite the pressure to reduce overheads inherent in a tight budget)'.

• 'Establishing an onsite office facility to accommodate the integrated project team was also important for ensuring integration'.

The project had a joint leadership team which consisted of the project director, construction contractors, design contractors, and other stakeholders. The main role of the joint leadership team was to establish and maintain a culture of **one team with a 'best for project' mindset.**

Chapter 13:

Conclusion

Infrastructure projects are a necessity for any country's economy, and the advancing economies, such as those of China, Brazil, India, and Saudi Arabia are investing huge sums into their infrastructure to advance their countries to become economic superpowers. The mega projects being constructed involve huge sums; errors in judgement in leading these projects can cause organisations to collapse and massive embarrassment to countries. However, many projects still go over budget and are also late, which should not be the norm in the industry. The reasons for this are sometimes many.

Although, this is never discussed as the reason for the project not being successful; however, do we really understand what success is? What is success and how do we judge success? Do we take the time to define what success means for every project? Do we take into consideration every stakeholders definition of success or do we think those don't matter because it is the client who is paying for the project?

Is success an illusion? How come some projects are said to be failures during the delivery stage and years down the line are seen as a huge success? Is it because the wrong benchmark criteria are used to judge success? Are the criteria for judging the success of stand-ard projects the same as those for judging large infrastructure pro-jects, which have a lot of public scrutiny and high media exposure? Shouldn't we tailor success criteria to suit the type of projects as we are supposed to do for all project management processes?

If we do not define what success is for a project from every stake-holder's point of view, then it is less likely that we will be able to de-fine the factors that will contribute to the success of the project even more so to large infrastructure projects.

What is sometimes called success is not necessarily project success, but project management delivery success. Sometimes we wrongly assume the project has failed when the project delivery stage seems not to meet our benchmarked success criteria. At times our bench-marked criteria of cost and schedule are wrongly set, which gives us the impression that we have failed at the delivery stage. However, not meeting a benchmarked cost or schedule does not necessarily mean the project is a failure as you need to wait for the benefits re-alisation stage.

Brunel's bridges and tunnels, Sydney Opera House, and the Channel Rail Link have shown that projects that were said to be failures at the delivery stage sometimes turn out to be a huge success.

Money is a huge behaviour influencer on large infrastructure pro-jects. Proper estimates should be developed to set the right budget and schedule and to prevent misconception of project failures. This will give the project a proper foundation for success. This requires strong leadership on large infrastructure projects which are normal-ly complex.

Also as the complexity of a project increases, the factors that make them successful requires a special type of leadership.

This book is written from a project manager's point of view, having gone through the frustrations and crisis of complex projects in several industries. Although we have discussed each factor on its own, there is a common thread between all of them, which is having the right kind of leadership on board. All the factors require leadership or are tools of leadership. This is how much the right type of leadership is essential for implementing complex infrastructure projects. For complex infrastructure projects, strong collaborative and servant leadership skills are crucial to success.

The principles in this book are not all the answers in completing a complex or large infrastructure project successfully. However, they are principles that have been proven to be either the reason for projects being successful or lessons learnt on projects which failed. There might be things that you have come across in this book that are new to you and others that you may know very well. The intention is to bring all the right principles together at one place to provoke your thoughts to research further and implement them. Remember that wisdom is knowledge applied; knowledge alone will not make your project successful. There is so much material out there — do your research, study, and apply what you learn.

Note that there is no silver bullet for ensuring complex or large infrastructure projects will be successful, as some books, processes, and theories try to proclaim. This book does not claim to be one that will quickly remove all your concerns and make your project fantastic. However, the book gives you some of the critical tools and prompts you on other research you can undertake to help develop yourself as a project leader so you can lead your project to success. As a project leader, you need to spend time researching, reading, and implementing the leadership theories that you learn. You will realise that some don't work for you, and soon you will develop your own style that is effective.

Remember that the contractor's definition of success may be different from that of the client. The client and contractor's definition of success may also be different from that of the delivery project manager. What the public sees as success may be skewed by what is presented to them by the media. Success is, therefore, a complex phenomenon in itself. Therefore, in delivering a large infrastructure project, one has to consider all these different perspectives and come up with acceptable success criteria. Then depending on the complexity of the project, one will need to come up with a recipe of the right mix of the success factors described in this book and tailor it to achieve their definition of success.

In life, our goal is to achieve mastery. Challenges come to help us in this. Therefore, chart your own course!

References

Books

1. *Emotional Capitalist — The New Leaders* (Martyn Newman)
2. *Touchpoints — Creating Powerful Leadership Connections in the Smallest of Moments* (Douglas Conant and Mette Norgaard)
3. *On Becoming a Leader* (Warren Bennis)
4. *Collaborative Leadership — Building relationships, Handling Conflicts and Sharing Control* (David Archer and Alex Cameron)
5. Agile Practice Guide
6. *Causation and Delay in Construction Disputes* (Nicholas J. Carnell)
7. *Construction Management and Organisational Behaviour* (Maureen Rhoden with Brian Cato)
8. *Rhetoric — A Very Short introduction* (Richard Toye)
9. *Total Construction Management — Lean Quality in Construction Project Delivery* (John S. Oakland and Marton Marosszeky)
10. *Principles and Power of Vision* (Dr Myles Munroe)

11. *The Power of Character in Leadership: How Values, Morals, Ethics and Principles Affect Leaders* (Dr Myles Munroe)

12. *The Toyota Way: 14 Management Principles from the World's Greatest Manufacturer* (Jeffrey K. Liker)

13. *Principles* (Ray Dalio)

14. *Mega Project Management — Lessons on Risk and Project Management from the Big Dig* (Virginia A. Greiman)

15. *Procuring Successful Mega-Projects — How to Establish Major Government Contracts without Ending up in Court* (Louise Hart)

16. *Industrial Megaprojects: Concepts, Strategies, and Practices for Success* (Edward W. Merrow, 2011)

17. *Managing Large Infrastructure Projects — Research on Best Practices and Lessons Learnt in Large Infrastructure Projects in Europe* (Marcel Hertogh, Stuart Baker, Pau Lian Staal-Ong, and Eddy Westerveld)

Other Publications

1. Crossrail project: the execution strategy for delivering London's Elizabeth line (William Tucker)

2. Crossrail legacy website

3. Megaprojects: The good, the bad and the better (Nicklas Garemo, Stefan Matzinger, and Robert Palter)

4. The London Olympics 2012 – A success story in Sustainable Infrastructure Development; Looking Beyond the Games (Joe Francica)

5. Ranking of System Implementation Success Factors (*Project Management Journal*) by James J Jiang, Gary Klein and Joseph Balloun

6. Project Success and Failure: What is success, what is failure and how can you improve your odds for success? (Robert Frese and Dr Vicki Sauter)

7. The Economic Benefits of Infrastructure Projects Procured with private Finance (Andrew W. Morley)

8. How to Motivate a team (SUSTAiN Factsheets)

9. Minding the 4 P's of Personality Styles (Tony DiLeonardi)

10. 4 Personality Types that all Leaders Should Learn to recognise (Crestcom Global)

11. Semantic Barriers to Communication (Aradhna Malik, Vinod Gupta School of Management, India Institute of Technology Kharagpur)

12. Communication: The Process, Barriers, and Improving Effectiveness (Fred C. Lunenburg, Sam Houston State University)

13. Plain English ISO 31000 2009 – Risk Management Dictionary

14. Top 10 myths of risk (APM Community, by David Hillson)

15. Risk Management for charities – Getting Started: supplementary guidance, Institute of Risk Management)

16. Rethinking Risk – Beyond the tick box (CFG, SAYER VINCENT)

17. Risk Management: Pro-active Principles for Project Success (Liz Markewicz and Don Restiano)

18. Project Interfaces (D. Antoniadis)

19. Planning, Scheduling, Monitoring and Control – The Practical Project Management of Time, Cost and Risk (APM-KNOWLEDGE)

20. Why your emotional Intelligence is more important than your IQ (Kathy M)

21. 5 ways to build a High-Performance team (Joseph Folkman)

22. Top 10 Main Causes of project Failure (Rosanne Lim)

23. "The Work of Leadership," *Harvard Business Review* (Ronald A Heifetz and Donal L Laurie)

24. Rescuing Troubled Projects (A TenStep White Paper)

25. Project Troubleshooting – Tiger teams for reactive risk management (Project Management Journal by Alex Pavlak)

26. Infrastructure Planning and Delivery – Best Practice Case Studies December 2010 (Australian Government – Department of Infrastructure and Transport

27. www.lean.org

28. Bob Emiliani article on is Lean the same as TPS published on April 3, 2016

29. Managing Integrated Project Delivery (Joel Darrington, Dennis Dunne and Will Lichtig)

30. "Introduction to Lean" (Lean Construction Institute)

31. Helm, J. & Remington, K. (2005). Effective project sponsorship: an evaluation of the role of the executive sponsor in complex infrastructure projects by senior project managers. Project Management Journal, 36(3), 51-61.

32. A risk-management approach to a successful infrastructure project by Frank Beckers and Uwe Stegemann (McKinsey & Company report November 2013)

33. The Art of Project Leadership: Delivering the World's Largest Projects (McKinsey Capital Projects & Infrastructure Practice September 2017)

34. Success Factors in Large Infrastructure Projects: The Contractor's Perspective (Master of Science Thesis in the Master's Programme Design and Construction Project Management – Tedh Adelback & Niclas Johansson)

35. The Failure of Metronet (Department for Transport – Report by the Comptroller and Auditor General, HC 512 Session 2008-2009, 5 June 2009

36. House of Commons Committee of Public Accounts; Department for Transport: The failure of Metronet. Fourteenth Report of Session 2009-10

37. A Risk-Management approach to a successful infrastructure project (Mc Kinsey & Company November 2013 Report by Frank Beckers and Uwe Stegemann

38. Incentives in Construction Contracts: Should we pay for Performance? By Will Hughes, Iyassu Yohannes and Jan-Betram Hillig

39. The art of project leadership: Delivering the World's largest projects – McKinsey Capital Projects & Infrastructure Practice September 2017

Printed in Great Britain
by Amazon

37608042R00143